All That I Am Is Here

A Story of Life, Love and Daily Living

by

Larry L. Hall Sr. Ph.D

authorHOUSE™

1663 LIBERTY DRIVE, SUITE 200
BLOOMINGTON, INDIANA 47403
(800) 839-8640
WWW.AUTHORHOUSE.COM

First published by AuthorHouse 03/10/05

ISBN: 1-4208-2260-8 (sc)

Printed in the United States of America
Bloomington, Indiana

This book is printed on acid-free paper.

Dedication

I dedicate this book to my family. For better or worse they made me what I am today. And to my prodogy for they will have to make the final decision on how I lived my life and how they feel about me.

Table of Contents

Dedication v

Preface: xi

Chapter 1 1
   My Childhood and Beyond 1
   My Brothers and Sisters 5
   High School 9
   My Parents..11
   My Grandparents 15
   My First Love 17
   My Musical Carreer..24
   My Live as a Railroad Employee 26
   True Friends..31
   My First Wife 34
   Try Again? 35
   Did I finally Find Her? 38

Chapter 2..40
   The Courtship as It wasn't..40

Chapter 3..42
   Living Together 42

Chapter 4..44
   The Arguments 44

Chapter 5..47
   Jealousy and Religion...47

Chapter 6..50
   More Arguments and my Mother's Death 50

Chapter 7..53
   My Fathers Death and My Marriage 53

Chapter 8..55
   Conflict Resolution..55

Chapter 9..61
   Children (Yours) 61
   Adult Children (Yours?) 65

Chapter 10..68
   The Career Widow...68

Chapter 11..72
   Priorities 72

Chapter 12..75
   The Right Priorities?..75

Chapter 13..77
   You and your Spouse After 40..................................77

Chapter 14..85
   Your love life after 40...85

Chapter 15..90
   Why your children don't understand your sexuality 90
   Why we don't understand our own sexuality 92

Chapter 17..96
   RE-Marriage 96

Chapter 18..105
   Surprises 105

Chapter 19..107
   Leadership as seen from the Middle 107
   What is True Leadership?..109
   Can Leaders be made?..110
   Are leaders created? 113
   Leadership Training in the workplace 118
   Leadership and Management.....................................124
   The feeling of the common employee 129

The Employer 137

The State of Business 139

Chapter 20..142

My Thoughts about other things..142

Right , Wrong and Making Choices 142

Would Jesus drive an SUV 153

The Rift between Science and Theology 157

Is there one true religion? 159

What is the difference between religion and faith? 161

Why Is Our Religion The Only Real One?..........................163

Why are we so intolerant of other religions?......................165

Why are some religions so violent?.....................................167

What can be done to fix the problem?..................................172

Should we all be just like Jesus? 173

Chapter 21 177

Now for a short discussion about Cloning 177

In Conclusion..180

Preface:

Please don't think that I know any more about life and living than you. It's just that I have made a lot of mistakes and want to maybe steer someone else away from the path that I may have taken earlier in my life. This book is not about sex although I will discuss it. It is not about the meaning of life, everyone has a different reason for being here. It also is not a how to manual on how to have a happy marriage, only you and your partner can make that happen but I have some ideas.

These pages are about *My Life*. I am writing this because I hope that any one who wanted to know what I was like could read these pages and see who or what I am or was. You don't have to read between the lines as I am a pretty straight forward person. The things I Believe and the things I have done are the proof that I am me. I am sure that I have the family trait of a conveint memory and all of the things I write are not as acurate as they could be but I tried to be as honest and straight forward as I can being me.

I try to make my marriage as much fun as it can be. I was requested to write this book by my wife and several of her friends so here is my attempt at conveying what I did to deserve the honor and maybe help someone else have fun too. FUN That is the Key. I told my wife when we married many years ago that life with me was not going to be easy but it would never be boring. Nothing makes me happier than to see my wife laugh. I hope you find some of the chapters of this book helpful, if not I hope you find them fun.

Chapter 1

My Childhood and Beyond

My Life at a young age

I don't remember much before I went to school but was told by my sisters that I was a terror. At the age of six weeks I had Spinal Menengitus and at nine years of age had Hepatitus. In both cases survival chances were at a minimum but somehow by the grace of god I made it through. Also at age four years old I was attached by my grandparents family dog and was hospitalized for a long time developing an alergy to pennicillin..

I was the ten year junior of my next sister and was (as I was told by my sisters) a burden to them. My mother worked from the time I can remember until her late fifties. I was home alone after my sister married, I was six or so. I can remember my mother getting me up at 5:30am when she and my father would leave for work and I would wait oo the sofa and some mornings I fell back asleep and others I found myself crying for her wanting her to be with me. I always seemed to make the school bus at 7:10 am and was at school around 7:45. School started at 8:20am sharp and this left some time for play. I didn't seem to enjoy this time with other children and for the sake of me I can't remember why. It always seemed that the other children looked at me differently and I couldn't figure it out. I now think that most of these memories may be a misinterpitation of what really happened but I still flet that way at the time. I had few friends and so I turned into a geek. I always blew the bell curve on all of the tests without even trying further exserbating the problem. It all seemed too easy for me and I didn't even have to try. Every day when I returned home from school at 3:45pm, I would go to the freezer and get a frozen hamburger patty and cook it for myself and watch television. This became a lifelong habbit for me that still goes today in various forms. I would wait for my parents to return home at 5:50PM every night like clockwork. My mother would fix what we called supper and then her and dad would go to their sofa's or chair and by 7:00pm they were both asleep. I would have control of the TV until bedtime which for me was abouot 10:00pm. I would wake my parents up sometime other times they would wake themselves up and they would then go to bed. Then they would rise at 4:30AM to start the whole day over. Sometimes I would awake early and hear them talking in the kitchen, most times about everyday things other times they would argue and fight. This routine continued for about ten more years.

I don't know if it was because I was lazy or because I had no other friends or interests but I always found myself very tired and sleepy by about 11:00 pm every night. When I got older this made for some early dates as I was getting sleepy about 10:30 and wanted to go home. I was what they now call a "Latch key kid.". although we didn't even lock our doors back then as our closest neighbor was about a quarter of a mile away. When I was about eight my closest friend lived about two miles from my home and when I got my first bike I was then able to spend time with him. His parents were almost the epitimy of what I thought parents should be. The father worked and the mother stayed home to be with the children and run the home. I think my judgement was skewed by the TV as I liked to watch "Ozzie and Harriet" and "Father Knows Best". His father was a gruff person and seemed to always to be in a bad mood. His mother on the other hand was a rather large woman with a sunny and compassionate disposition. I spent a lot of time with them and when I was eight or nine my parents decided that I needed someone to watch me during the summer months when I wasn't in school so they hired my friend's mother. I enjoyed these summers and looked forward to going to my friend's house. As I grew older I started to take care of myself during the summer months and actually earned some money doing farm work. I hauled hay and shoveled chicken manure into spreaders for about $1.00 per hour. This was hard work but made me appreciate what my parents had to do to provide for me.Then when I was fifteen I got my first real job. I went to work for the city of Dalton painting fire hydrants. We were given a drop cloth a wire brush and a gallon of paint and directed where to paint. We walked the whole city of Dalton that year painting 356 Fire hydrants.

Birthdays

I am sure that my parents had birthday parties for me when I was young but I can't remember. I do remember that it seemed that on every birthday my parents would give me something usually money for my birthday. I however rememer when I was sixteen years old my girlfriend had a party for me. I felt uncomfortable because most of the people there were her friends. My best friend didn't show because he and his girlfriend decided to go parking instead. It may seem that I am giving the impression that my childhood was unhappy. Nothing could be further from the truth. I had a freedom and hapiness that today's children miss. I could ride my bike without fear of being hurrassed by gangs or cars (to a large extent). I could explore the countryside and swim in the ponds and lakes as I wanted. I found that reading was not a chore but a joy. I had few friends but we always seemed to have a good time when we were together. My parents loved me and did the best they could and I now realize all of the sacrifices they made for me. I miss them both deeply.

My Brothers and Sisters

I have two brothers and two sisters who were not around much when I was young. The youngest being ten years my senior. I will have to say that the relationship we have had over the years seems a little different from what I thought brothers and sisters should be. My sisters I am sure loved me but I was probably too young to notice. My youngest memories of my siblings was of my next sister. It seem I was always in the way as little brothers were apt to be when teenage girls are dating. I tended to destroy all of her possessions and made a resident nusiance of myself.

Here is a story related to me by them. There was a small creek behind our house and we were told not to go there without our parents. My sisters would sometimes take me and we would go without permission when our parents were at work. Of course I was told not to tell them we went and so invariably I would say something like "We didn't go to the creek today and swim." Of course alerting our parents that we did. Another time when I was small and still in diapers my sisters and their dates had taken me to the skating rink in our hometwon and when I went to the restroom I came out swinging my diaper and naked for all of the world to see. It seems that one of the dates of my sister made an unkind comment about me and she got very angry at him. I however don't remember any of this but I can believe it was true.

Things get a little bit stranger with the older brothers. My oldest brother had a son that was only two years younger than me.

This made my brother feel he was more of a parent to me than a brother. He felt he had the right to dicipline me whenever he felt it necessary. I resented this. I know he felt he was doing the right thing but looking back I needed a brother not another parent. My next brother was the pride and joy of the family. When he was young he joined the navy. One of the fondest memories I have of him is when he would visit us on leave and he brought me a plastic model of a ship. It wasn't his ship but I could have cared less. When he returned from the navy he was married and had a baby girl. He joined the police force in our town and started college. He was as far as I know the first of our immediate family to go to college. He finally received his associates degree in business administration and my parents were so proud. From the time he returned from the navy he was held to me as the person to emulate. Forget that we were nothing alike. I was told "Why can't you be more like your brother?" I didn't see him then as a brother but as a rival. I would someday prove that I was as good as he was. This would shadow my life for the next fifteen years. My brother was becoming a big success in my parent's eyes. He started a business and was growing in wealth. Forget that he had been married three times and had other problems that I won't discuss in this book. All I heard was "Look what your brother is doing now." I will not disagree that my brother has had success and in the last several years has become more spritual, but I know for a fact that he has the 'Hall Trait' of a convenient memory. I remember when our mother died in 1980 and we were staying late at the funeral home we talked for a little bit and he was at that time I believe an agnostic.

He said to me that "When you were dead you were dead." I found this strange as our parents while not regular church goers were very spritual people. When I reminded him of these comments years later he says he never in his life would say such a thing. This happens a lot when any Hall is reminded of things he would rather forget. But maybe I am being just a little too critical. I will probably do the same thing when I am in that situation. I competed with my brother for a lot of years. Even as an adult I felt I was being preasured to live up to what he represented. Even after I married he was still held up to me as a role model. My wife resented my brother for a lot of years because it seemed (mayby only to her) that my brother took every occasion to make me feel unsuccessful or small because I was not following in his percieved footsteps. I will disclose a situation in high school later in this book relating to this situation. I am sure that my brother felt that he was just giving me an insentive to do better but I didn't see it that way. I felt that he was rubbing his success in my face and saying "See you can't do this." I discovered in my late twenties that I was a fool to feel this way. I found a self worth that actually made me feel sorry for my brother which was also the wrong thing. I realized that I was doing all of the right things for all of the wrong reasons. I wanted to be a success not because I wanted to do better for my family but to prove to my brothers and sisters that I was as good and successful as they were. I can't remember why I felt this way with my sisters as as far as I can remember they never made me feel bad or unsuccessful. The main reason for this I believe is thay had their own families to take care of and just didn't have the time.I know they love me now but I didn't see it then. I have related in this book that we were a close family and I believe it with all of my heart. Not close in years but close in heart. We would do anything for each other and we all love each other very much. I am sure that they feel that I was probably spoiled as a child and as far as it goes I may have been. However now I am at a stage in my life where I am happy and looking forward to what the future has to hold. I have given up all of the old resentments (founded or unfounded) and can now feel closer to them than ever before. I now judge my success by a new set of standards. Standards that I set for myself. No one will ever be able to make me feel that I am unworthy of love or respect again. I have a new sense of self worth and am grateful for all of the opportunities I have had over the years.

High School

I was a social outcast at my high school and I didn't understand why for a long time. I have very few good memories of my life from thirteen to seventeen. I was small and meek (another word for scared or cowardly), and was picked on by a lot of people whose names are written in my mind forever (just kidding). I was also somewhat intelligent another fatal flaw if you want to be popular without being on a sports team. I had an IQ of 146 (Why wasn't I told at the time) and the common sense of a tomato. I was too small to play sports however since my older brother was on the first football team the high school had he pressured me into playing football and when I wanted to quit he talked the coach into giving me another chance (Why Me..) so for the rest of the year I sat on the bench (Thank God). I however was no great scholar as most of the time I was bored with what the teachers were teaching. So for the next four years I was open game for any girl that wanted to make fun of me and every jock or jock wanta-be to get points for making someone else look stupid or weak. I never stood up for myself maybe because I was weak. I had no self confidence or sense of self worth and it was my fault. I blame no one for my short comings then or now. I have learned with experience that most of the popular kids and jocks were probably more insecure than me or just plain stupid. Most now have the Georgia Redneck Dream (a double wide trailer, a pregnant wife with 2 kids and a Trans-am). Seriously I hold no grudges now as I have learned that pent up anger and resentment doesn't hurt them, only me. I however did have my first true love in high school but I digress.

So Much for High School. How about college you say? Well I went to college at a local two year junior college for about a year. I didn't have any better time there except most of the kids were too busy trying to do well that they didn't have time to make trouble for me. Or this is how I perceived it (Pretty Pitiful Huh…). Don't feel sorry for me. I had two great parents who had no understanding of me but were great anyway as they supported me as much as I would let them. I had two brothers and two sisters, the youngest ten years my elder. and four other siblings that were deceased before I was born.

My Parents

I feel that children don't have a sense of what a parent is until they are grown. My parents didn't have a scholastic education. My father made it to the sixth grade and my mother to the fourth. This gave me an unjustified sense of superority when I was a teenager. The memories of my father are of a man with problems, strength and understanding. He successfully beat a drinking problem and was a good provider. He worked in a Carpet mill most of my life and worked ten or more hours a day as long as I could remember. My father was in his early fourties when I was born and my mother was almost fourty. I am sure that this put stress on their marriage and my mother's health. I was a sickly child and this couldn't have helped. My earliest memories of my father were when he would come home and we would sit in a chair and watch Television together(I was probably four or so). He would sometimes bring me a candy bar and we would watch westerns (his favorite) untill we went to bed. My earliest memories of my mother are vauge. I remember her holding me while I went to sleep and she was talking to other people in our living room. Other memories were not so warm. I remember my mother having problems with her temper and taking medicine that made her sleep a lot. It came to pass that she had to be hospitalized for a nervous breakdown and went to a hospital in Atlanta for several months. Dad and I would visit and I remember mom giving me Danish Wedding Cookies (a favorite of mine today) while she visited with dad. I much later found out that she was getting electroshock treatments. I had no understanding of what was going on and when I finally realized the depth of her problem I felt somehow responsible. I am sure that my father suffered along with her and this made things even more difficult for them. When mom came home things seemed better. Mom was never the same but I grew accustomed to her new ways.

When I became a teenager I am sure that I tested their patience. As a teenager I felt superior to my parents because I was now in the tenth grade and had surpassed them in education. I was wrong but no one could make me believe that. My mom always inrtoduced me as her baby even when I was six inches taller than her. My mom was all of five foott three inches and had an attitude that wouldn't stop. She had only one indulgance that I knew of. Every Saturday morning she would go to her hair dresser downtown and have her hair washed and fixed. To me her hair always looked the same but I think she just liked to have other adults to talk to that weren't related to her. She was a good cook and we as a family usually had Sunday coffee if not breakfast together. The Sunday morning get togethers were one of the highlights of the week for mom and dad. All of the married children would come and sit around the kitchen table and talk. I was never intentionaly excluded but everyone thought of me as a child and didn't pay much attention to me but I still liked that everyone was there. As a rural family most of the children lived less than ten miles from Mom and Dad so could visit frequently. This added to us being a close family.

Holidays were always a family gathering and everyone brought something different to eat. My mother would make her famous Spagetti and My sister-in-law would make the Pecan Pie. This is as it should be and I am sure that most families have something of the same experiences.

My father was a good man. He worked hard and enjoyed life as much as he could. I can remember my father sitting on the sofa after one Christrmas morning giving a diatribe of how my mother's Volkswagon Beetle had hit a small dog while he was driving it and the dog walked away after the collision because the car was not big enough to hurt it. He went on for twenty minutes and I laughed so hard I cried. At the age of fifty-five my father could still outrun me in a footrace. He had his health problems such as alchol earlier in his life and diabetes later but he never complained and always tried to make me a better person by showing his courage. My father never played sports or went camping or fishing with me but I wasn't interested in those things anyway. He impressed the value of an education and how I was to judge people. He impressed that you are known by the people you associate with. I was taught not to judge a person until I got to know them and that lumping a group of people into a stereotype was not only foolish but just plain stupid. As I had very few friends this was not evident to me at the time. My Parents worked hard and long to make my life better that theirs had been. I am what I am because of them. I hope I pass the same values to my children and grandchildren.

I don't know if I did all of the things in high school to make my parents proud or to show my brother I could succeed without him or his help. I was a good student and made A's and B's without much effort. I was president of the science club for three years, In 4-H, The Ecology Club, The Yearbook Staff, and The Latin Club. I got my first college scholarship for public speaking from Junior Acheivement and was asked to speak for a small fee at several local club lunches (Ruritans, VFW etc.). Needless to say my parents were the most influencial people in my life and I hope I have made them proud and have my children understand what they were like.

My Grandparents

I don' have many memories of my Grandparents. My Mother's Father and Step-mother lived in Kentucky and we only visited them four times in my life. I however did discover where my mother got her attitude. My Grandfather Roberts was a very rough and opinionated man. My step-grandmother on the other hand seemed gentle and very loving. I didn't get to spend much time with them and am sorry I didn't get to know them better.

My father's parents were on the other hand were close and we went to visit them almost every Sunday morning until my grandfather's death. I remember they lived close to a railroad and I enjoyed collecting railroad spikes.My grandfather also had some chicken houses and I got into trouble for scaring the chickens.

My grandparents would sit on this old sofa together and everyone knew not to sit in their place. We had many luncheons at their home as they had a screened in back porch where we ate. When my Grandfather died suddenly we stopped going as much. We then started gathering at our house on Sunday Morniing. My grand mother lived another several years and the last three were racked by the pain of spinal cancer. She finally got to the point that when I visited she thought I was my father and would ask about Sadie and the kids. I contributed this to all of the pain medication she was on and understood. I have Aunts on my father's side, three of whom never married and who cared for my grandparents until their death and still live in the same house that they shared for all of those years.

15

Since that time one has passed but the others still live there. I visit from time to time and they seem happy.

My First Love

I was fifteen and on a trip with the Junior Achievement group to Nashville, Tennessee. I fell in with a group of geeks (as they were called at the time) and was having a good time. Then I noticed a girl. She was sitting with a group of what I perceived to be Egg Heads. She didn't smile at me but she didn't laugh when I said "HI" either (a total success in my book). So I asked her name. She told me and I asked which school she was from. She said Dalton High School. This frightened me a little. Dalton High was the school most of the rich kids in the county went to, but at least she didn't go to my school and know anything about me. I asked to sit by her and she said Ok. We started to talk and things went from good to better. For the first time in my life I felt not like a winner but not like a looser. The three day trip culminated at the last hour of the trip home I gathered enough courage to kiss her. Not exactly my first kiss but the best I could remember and it lasted all of 3 seconds. When we returned to Dalton I had a new sense of elation and a phone number. We spoke on the phone for several weeks before I could get up the nerve to ask her to meet me at the movies for a date. She informed me that she could not date but could meet me at the movies with a girlfriend. This was good for me. I arranged to meet her in front of the movie at 1:00PM on a Saturday. Being 15 I had a learner's permit to drive and my father let me drive to the movie theater in our 65 Plymouth Fury III as far as I was concerned the coolest car on the road. This was 1969. Arriving at the movie I saw her. My heart was pounding so hard I was sure she could see my chest jump. Her and her Girlfriend (I found out later it was her younger cousin) already had tickets and were ready. I can't remember the movie but I remember everything she wore and what she smelled like, to this day the smell of strawberry musk makes me feel warm and nervous at the same time. It took me about an hour to put my arm around her and in doing so I trapped her hair between the top of the seat and my arm so when she moved it pulled her hair (So Much for my first smooth move). The movie was over in 5 minutes (time flies and so forth). When I asked her if I could see her again , Expecting "No. I don't think we have anything in common." She said to call her, so 15 minutes after I got home I called her and wanted to know when I could see her. The answer was her parents needed to meet my parents. Horror of Horrors, was this to be the end. To me it seemed that my parents were hillbillies because my mother had a 4th grade education and my father a 6th Grade, But no risk was enough to curb my adolescent fervor. I let My Mom talk to her Mom and they talked way too long for my srnse of well being but it was all set. Next Saturday evening we were to get together at her home for the meeting of my life. Next Saturday I was a wreck but we went and arrived at their home about 7:00pm. Their house wasn't any better or larger than our house but when we went in it hit me like a brick. Man they had air conditioning. We had a window Air conditioner but this was something new. The whole house (as much as I saw) was the same temperature. I knew we were in over our heads then. When she introduced me to her mother as expected I introduced my parents to her mother. All seemed well. The evening went off without a hitch as far as I know. They sent us into the den to watch television while they talked. This went on for over 2 hours. I later found out that my dad had done this so I could visit with "My little friend" a little longer, What a Guy! When we left I felt as though a Buick was lifted from my chest. The next day I called and was told that her mother liked my parents and that we would be able to see each other again. I asked her when would be a good time and we set a time for me to spend some time with her at her house. This went on for a long time. I turned sixteen and got my driver license on my birthday. I passed my written test with a 100 and then passed my driver test. I felt like a man then. But when I called my girl (that's what she was by then) she said that we still would have to wait for her sixteenth birthday to date with a car. Her birthday was over a month away. I was heartbroken. When she turned sixteen I went to her birthday party. This was to be a culture shock for me. Here I was a boy from the country and there she was with all of her friends from some of the most prestigious homes in Dalton. I really felt out of place, but to her credit she did her best to make me part of the group and for this I will be always grateful. Then came the fateful night, we had a date to go to dinner alone. I went to pick her up in my car and the first thing I did was to scrape the tailpipe on the car entering her driveway. I was later to find out that entering and exiting her driveway was an art in itself. I think this was a plot to tell them when we came and went (Paranoid Too.). The appointed time was 7:00 PM and was then told she had to be home by 10:00PM at the latest. I thought this was a test, but later realized that this would be the norm. We dated for two more years, spending as much time with each other as possible. We went through our high school years together. I guess I was too comfortable. Now we come to the first discussion of sex. I was sixteen and very anxious about sex. I knew what the feelings were but I had no outlet. See sex was for after marriage. As it was discussed back then there are two kinds of girls' yada yada yada. I wanted the right kind of girl for my wife, so that left my main girl out of the picture (As if I would never try anything with her, what planet did I live on?). So I made a big mistake. While my girl was gone to visit her aunt I was invited by another girl to go to the movies. This girl meant nothing to me and maybe I hoped I would get lucky. So I picked her up and she wanted to go to the Drive-in Movie. This girl while not overly attractive wasn't unattractive. But a funny thing happened. I felt uncomfortable with this girl and never tried anything. However someone else must have seen me there with this girl and when my girl returned she thought I had done something I hadn't. As most men know telling a girl that she was wrong is almost an impossibility. I could not convince her that nothing happened so I did what any man in my position would do. I begged like a mother for forgiveness. This is hindsight might have been a mistake. Life with my girl after that seemed to be a list of suspicions and stress. About six months of this and things settled back to normal. I then managed to get the nerve to ask her to marry me when we graduated from High School. She said "Yes" and life truly began, or at least I thought so. Then something unexpected happened. I didn't mind that her mother was planning our future for us, or that we were going to our hometown junior college together, I didn't even mind the custom ties for all occasions her and her mother made to match her formal gowns, no not that. This really came out of left field. I was the family driver for my nephews and nieces who were from ten to thirteen years of age. The County Fair came to town and I made arrangements to take my girl and my nephew and a couple of friends to the fair. Picking up my nephew and two of his friends we continued to the home of my beloved. We pulled up into the driveway and when I knocked on the door was confronted by my girlfriend and her mother. I was told in no uncertain terms that her daughter was not going to be seen in a car with any black children. Quote" It is bad enough she has to go to school with them. She doesn't have to socialize with them." I was stunned to say the least. I don't think that my girl or her parents had the same prejudices but she said I had to make a choice between them and her. I got back in my car not knowing what to do and dropped the kids off at the fair. I could not comprehend what the little twelve year old boy could have done to deserve that attitude. I had to make a choice? It didn't seem right. I called my girl back and said "Tell your mother that I couldn't do that to any kid and that I guess that we (meaning her mother) could not be friends." This was taken by my girl as me telling her that the black child was more important than her. She never realized that I was only talking about her mother and not her. I was told later that she cried for hours. When her mother called my Sister to find out how I could do this to her daughter my sister told her that we were taught to treat everybody the same until we knew them well enough to make a decision on what kind of people they were regardless of color. I think this made the situation worse. I was heartbroken when the day after she wouldn't even take my phone calls. I tried for days until she finally conceded to meet with me in her living room. I arrived and we sat on the sofa. I tried to explain what happened, but she did not want to hear what I had to say except I was wrong and wouldn't do any such thing again. I guess I was weak willed again and did just exactly what she expected. The next spring came graduation. It was one of the crowning points of my life so far. My parents were proud and I had a scholarship to college for $450.00 or about two quarters of tuition and books. I had a job with the city of Dalton reading meters. I think I got this job because of my future father-in-law as he worked there. My girl got a job at an accounting office as a receptionist. Then we had an argument. Now I can't even remember what the argument was about but I am sure that it was something small but we decided to seperate. I was heartbroken and nothing seemed to matter. I didn't want to go to school because she was there. I didn't want to work because I would see her father. I was totally lost. I ended up losing my job and dropping out of college after only three Quarters. It would be years before I would go back to school. This was the worst time of my life up to now or so I thought at the time. I felt alone and hopeless and could not be consoled by anyone. Everyone seemed concerned and wanted to do something but only time would heal this wound. Even today I find myself wondering where she is, What she is doing and if she can remember me with any affection.

Women please forgive a man if he has trouble trying to forget his first love for you never love as deeply or hurt as badly as the first time. Don't misunderstand, my wife means more to me than any other woman could but the "DREAM" never truly dies.

My Musical Carreer

When I was in High School I found out that I had a natural talent for the drums and joined a local band. I am sure that almost everyone joined a band at one time or another when they were young. We played School Dances (However none at My School) and Private Functions and were pretty good. I could sing a little and also learned to play the Guitar a little when necessary. I still carry the love for music today as I use my computer to compopse and record my music (Only for very special occasions). I kept up for several years and while I was working for the Railroad in Atlanta Ga. I was at a club on the north side of town in Kennesaw GA one night when the band playing there I foolishly mentioned to a friend that the drummer was terrible and I could do better. I don't know wheither my friend was trying to help me or embarass me but he told the band leader my comment and I was therefore called on my statement. I was shocked but too embarassed not to try. I soon discovered that this was fun. I finished two songs and returnd to my table. A week later the band leader called and offered me the job as drummer three nights a week. I explained that I couldn't work weekends and he didn't understand, but as I would accept a smaller fee we worked it out. About five months later as I was taking a break from playing at the club a gentleman came by and offered me his card. He worked for RCA Records in Atlanta and needed a studio drummer. He was offering Union Scale (about 17.50 per hour) and three days later I went to his office and agreed to work for them. One reason I went to work for them was they let me set my own schedule for the most part. I could come in at night and work three or four hours and do this whenever they needed me. I really never got to meet many recording stars but I met a few. Two years later I had to stop as my wife stated that it was the wrong thing to do while having a family and so my musical carreer was at an end. However I never witnessed any of the things I was warned of in the music industry such as drugs or loose women. Most of the people I had dealings with were professionals and content to be that way. If I had the courage at that time to fight for what I wanted my life might have taken a different path but who knows.

My Live as a Railroad Employee

I spent almost fourteen Years working for the Railroad. I started as a carpenter's helper on a bridge and building gang on the L&N Railroad. I was stationed on the Atlanta Division which covered from South Atlanta to North Chattanooga TN. I think I was hired basicly because the foreman of the gang was my father-in-law and he recommended me for the job. This caused some initial problems as the other people on the gang figured that I could do anything I wanted and no one had better say anything about it of they would be in trouble. After a few months the problem went away as they got to know who I was and where I was coming from. It was a good paying job and I actualy enjoyed most of the work. It wasn't long before I was a union carpenter and was givem more responsibility. When I had shown an apptitude for paperwork I was given the paperwork for the gang and I learned a lot about projects and how to schedule men and machines. The foreman of the gang being my father-in law felt it was alright to let me do the paperwork he was supposed to do and I didn't mind. My father-in-law had a drinking problem and we in the gang found ourselves taking care of him so he didn't get fired as this was the only life he had known, going to work for the railroad at age sixteen and being in his mid fifties now. After about eight years of working with the gang I bid on a job involving operating an eighty ton crane. I got the job and was trained in using various heavy machinery such as backhoes and dosers as well as cranes and pile drivers. The pay was better but it involved travel. I spent an average of nine months a year away from home. This is not condusive to a happy wife and children, but she endured it because we needed every penny we could get. I spent a lot of time away from home reading and learning new things. This is when I got my first computer but more about that later. The people I worked with were a strange lot. A great bunch of guys but being a railroad employee made for some strange circumstances. We shared a modified box car as a home. It was for the most comfortable except in the deep of winter or the heat of summer. Being in such close quarters will inevitably draw a group of people together or drive them to homicide. I soon began to think of most of these guys as a sort of extended family. We looked out for each other and had a lot of fun doing such simple things as playing football or video games. We ate, watched TV and slept in close quarters for three or four days a week. There are probably a lot of stories that I could tell about my experiences with these people but that would be another whole book. The turning point was the last five years I worked for the CSX Corp. who purchase the railroad and changed everything. The company wasn't exactly making a lot of money and they figured that all of the employees were not doing their best. We were taking advantage of the company and we were to be told how many people were waiting to take our jobs if we couldn't do better. I was so bad that when we were working and stopped for lunch on the job site because we didn't have time to go and buy lunch in thirty miunets that we spent an extra ten miunets at lunch and when the division supervisor found out placed a formal repremand in our files for wasting the companies time. The last straw was when my father was in the hospital in Atlanta suffering from a heart attack and I was called to come. I was putting the crane I was operating on the side track when the division supervisor drove up and asked me what I was doing. When I told him he asked if I didn't have any other brothers or sisters that could go in my place so I could continue working. I was stunned to say the least. A coworker with me looked at me and said "Just don't hit him. We'll take care of him you go on." I knew then that if this was how the company felt about me I was through worring about doing a good job for them and would take every opportunity to do as little as possible while I looked for another job.   Computers had been a hobby for me for about four years and I was very interested in them . I had become somewhat of a lengend (unearned) with my associates as a computer guru. It all began in Cartersville Ga when a mainframe terminal was having problems and the IBM repairman had been there all morning. He went to lunch and we arrived for lunch. I being interested in computers and electronics just had to take a look at what was going on. I notices a wire on the serial cable bent and when I picked it up it broke in two. Being me I rejoined the two wires and the terminl came up immediately. Of course my fellow associates had to make a big deal and the story grew from that. I can't say I didn't enjoy the notirioty. I then figured that I would try to get a job with them working on their computers but was told that they didn't hire anyone for the computer department without a college degree in computers. I had earlier purchased my first computer a COMMADORE VIC 20. I had learned a lot about it when I had a near fatal accident. Moving my crane from one city to another the line on my kerosene heater broke and my campcar burned with all of my belongings inside. I was partialy reimbursed and purchased my second computer a COMMADORE 64. I learned even more about them and learned to hack computers and programs as well as how to program them. I had at this time made friends with a gentleman who owned a computer store and he was more than helpful. I started spending all of my free time at the shop with him learning what I could and seeing the newest hardware and software. I even got a few programming jobs from him and his clients which inspired me even more. I was however neglecting my family and I justified it at the time by saying I was trying to better myself for the benefit of the whole family. Eventualy this was true but at the time it was just a line I used to get to do what I wanted. This all eventualy led to me leaving the railroad and with the support of my wife returning to work allowed me to chase the dream of working in the field of computers. But back to the railroad. I was starting to feel that I had wasted the years on the railroad and sometimes I would get physicaly ill when I had to go to work. I hated the job and the people I worked for. I felt used and abused by a corporation looking only at the bottom line and for the most part I was right. I loved the guys I worked with like brothers and knew I would miss them most of all but I had to do what I felt was right for me. So I took a three months leave of absence and tried my hand at computer work. My wife was happy that I wanted to leave the railroad and worked hard so I could try this dream. After three months I felt I could do this and was offered a job by a company in Dalton to repair and maybe work up to programming computers. I tendered my resignation to the railroad and felt good. For about three months after that I received a weekly call from my old division supervisor asking me to return to my job and I would not loose any of my senority or benefits. I wasn't interested and told him so on various occasions. It seems that the Crane I was operating was old and only two people in the US could operate it. Me and the gentleman who trained me before he retired at age 65 two years earlier. They had to scrap the crane as the next guy to try and use it ending up destroying the transmission and doing several hundred thousand dollars in damage to a bridge. The total cost was about two million dollars give or take some. This somehow made me feel good. It took me several years and enormous amount of training before I was making again what I made on the railroad when I left but now I feel much better about what I do and my life.

True Friends

I can count the true friends I have had on my fingers of one hand. I certainly have a lot of friends and aquaintances but only a few true friends. Like everyone else I have had good friends who later in our lives moved away from us either in distance or in personal closeness. A true friend no matter how far from you shows the same traits. They are loyal and may think of you as part of their extended family. I bring this subject up because so many of our so called friends are there for you when you least need them and make themselves unavaliable when real trouble comes to call. I see my children's friends are there only when there is fun to be had but when something serious happens that are not to be found or have an excuse not to be there. Some will even blame my children for things they have done. This shows a total lack of personal responsibility and character. I know these are outdated traits but they are what I look for.

There is one friend I must mention here. I have gone out of my way not to use names in this writing because I don't feel I have the right to name names or place anyone in a situation that they might feel uncomfortable. The man I have the most respect for after my father is Rabbi Zvi Ettinger. I was inrtoduced to this man at the computer shop I worked for and from that day on he was a major influence in my future decisions. I was a little apprehensive a first not knowing anything about the jewish faith and was sure I was going to do something that would turn every jewish person in town against

31

me. These are the fears of a person who has no inkling of other religions and the fear of the unknown breeds unwarranted fear and sometimes undeserved animosity. I was invited to his office at the temple and boy was I nervous. It turned out that he did everything he could to make me comfortable and I was enjoying myself soon after our first meeting. We sat sometimes for hours discussing everything from politics to computers (our favorite subject). He knew a lot of local business owners and through him I met some very infulential and interesting people. One of the programs I was most proud of was a jewish word processor I had written for him. I remapped the keyboard and programmed the printing fron left to right and could do a screen print. I also later wrote a program for his congregation and sold copies to other synagogues and was written about in a prominent jewish magazine. This is one of the few men who seemd to recongnize a potential in me that even I didn't see. He encouraged me and heaped praise and admiration on me even when I probably didn't deserve it. He showed me that nothing is beyond your reach if you are willing to work hard and long enough for it. He was one of my staunchest defenders and mentors. Why he took a liking to me I can't say but I thank god for him and his wisdom. He was a realist and didn't try to convince me that I would someday be rich or famous but that I was important to a lot of people and no person can be a failure if he has done his best. He took an interest in my family also and we all loved him. He loved all children but he made my children feel as if he was a long lost relative and he always had time to talk to the children no matter how busy he was. I was stunned when after ten years at the synagogue he was moving to Florida. I have seen him a few times since he moved and have always been very happy to see him and his family.

My First Wife

After my heartbreak with my first love I was dispondant. I figured I could not be complete without a mate (a mistake). So I fell for the first Girl that showed me any attention at all. I met this girl and was married within six months (Stupid I Know.). Still being a virgin at the time I thought this was my only outlet for sex. I went into this marriage blind, deaf, stupid, and horny. It took us a few minutes to figure out the equipment as neither one of us had any former experience. After a break in period of about an hour it seemed we were at it several times a day for about a month. Then we tapered down to about once a day, then once every other day. Then just when we felt like it. After about six months of this kind of marriage I think she figured there had to be something better and left me. Again I asked myself, where did I fail? The answer is I didn't, we were both too young and immature to undertake such a commitment. Not saying other people couldn't do it but this was me. There were no children or property and we separated amiably so no harm no foul. But Wait until wife two.

Try Again?

Several months after my divorce I met a woman senior my age by four years (at twenty three this amount seemed large). She was already divorced and had a son by another man. I wasn't going to make the same mistake again. I dated her for twelve months. About the ten Month she decided that we could be intimate at my home (I had a Trailer by myself by then. High on the hog huh…). After that I felt that it was my responsibility to make an honest woman of her. About a month before the wedding I was having serious doubts if I was doing the right thing and wanted to back out, but when I tried to discuss this with her she broke into tears and my resolve melted. We married on a Saturday and moved into my place with a four year old boy. We went along for about a year when my first child was born to us, a boy. Of course I named him Larry Junior after me. Things were moving fine. I had a job with the Railroad on the bridge gang. The job kept me away from home about six to nine months of the year. I would come home on Friday evening and Leave Monday morning early. I sometimes came home on Wednesday but not every week. This worked fine for use for about four years. Then it happened again. I won't go into details because I have no wish to relive what happened. It's something I'm not proud of and I know I was as much responsible as anyone for the situation. Let's just say I was caught up in a bad situation not completely of my own design. One affair by me later and upon meeting my current wife (Not the Affair) we were divorced. Then the usual thing happened

35

as does these things. My ex-wife decided that everything was my fault and her lawyer convinced a judge that I was always having an affair with another woman through the whole of our marriage even if she could'nt prove it. I guess the judge agreed with her so she got almost everything(Which wasn't much). The money in savings, The only car we had, my 35 MM Camera (which she didn't know how to use), $100 per week Child Support (I made $258 per week) all the furniture, and it felt like one of my testes. I got to be a part-time father, every other weekend, one week in the summer (whenever she wanted me to have him) and half the Christmas Holidays (which meant anytime after Christmas day) not to exceed two days. A Little later her new friend moved into the house and let me know in no uncertain terms that I was not welcome and would pick my son up on the street. This would be a fourteen year constant aggravation. Later that year I was injured at work and had to have surgery on my knee. She swore a warrant for my arrest for non-support. Posting Bail and arriving at court she was given another half of the settlement from the insurance company on my injuries. Then I had a stroke of luck? When my son turned fourteen he decided he would come and live with me and my wife. We embraced him and he joined the other three children we had. She signed custody over to us and we were happy, or so we thought. Three years and ten months later after the fourth time my Ex-wife was abused by her then husband (number three also) she called our son and asked him to come and stay with her. Our son was in his junior year of high school and had less than three months left. We thought he should wait until school was out.

Two nights later he ran away to be with his mother leaving us a note telling us she needed him more than he needed an education and he would continue school where she was. We reported him as a run away to the police to be told that he could do whatever he wanted and we had no recourse. Three months later I was summoned to court for non-support. My ex-wife had found a lawyer that would fight for her rights. She asked for almost four years back child support. It seems that there was an error on the paperwork filed with the court and she still had legal custody of our son. The judge found in her favor for the amount of $10,800, legal fees and court costs. I had three days to come up with $3000 or go to jail. I had to borrow the money. To add insult to injury the court ordered that my paycheck would be garnished for the weekly child support until the amount was paid in full. My ex-wife thought this was just and right. The next week she was arrested for Drunk driving and my son six months later married a girl already pregnant with his child. I paid child support for another three years and he saw none of it. His mother is now with a long-haul trucker and is seldom in the area to see our granddaughter who is now ten years old and beautiful. I hold no animosity for this woman and I hope that her life will be resolved in a manner that makes her happy. If everyone could find the kind of happiness I have found then most of the problems of the world would be small and solvable. I know that this seems too simplistic and it probably is, but happiness cannot be bought, rented, stolen or given, it must come from within. If your are looking for someone to make you happy you will never have true happiness or peace.

Did I finally Find Her?

Just when I thought I was getting somewhere my mother passed away suddenly. I was devastated and it seemed that my wife had suddenly become the most consoling person I knew. She may have only done simple things like hold my hand or talk to me but it seemed the world was crashing in and she was holding it on her shoulders. She would hold me at night and say nothing, but I knew that she truly loved me because all of the people I had loved until then ran at the first sign of trouble. It seem a shame that it would take something like this to make a man see the truth but if my mothers death had any reason I am sure now that she saved me from being alone and scared as she had always done. The arguments seemed to diminish probably because I had a good idea of what was important to me and money was way down on the list. This was the Beginning. But I get ahead of myself.

March 1980 I moved in to an apartment with a young woman. She was pretty and had an attitude (that is an understatement). I was finally becoming an adult. A least I thought so at the time. She had a daughter about four months old. How she came to be divorced we won't discuss as this has no bearing on my story. We enjoyed each other's company. My mother thought she was a little sleazy but came around in time. My father liked her from the beginning, my brothers and sisters just tolerated her. They said if I loved her so much that they could put up with her (gracious I guess.) I was still working for the railroad and going to school whenever and wherever

I could. We were married On Saturday September 27, 1980 at the Courthouse in Ringgold Georgia. I borrowed the $50 to get married on from a friend. She wore a peach gown and I wore a white shirt and tie. She had peach roses in a bouquet and my best friend and his third wife were in attendance as well as my small son.

Chapter 2

The Courtship as It wasn't

Shortly after we moved into the apartment we discovered why we were so hard to live with. We each had our routines and hated to have them upset. I hate to get up early and she wants to get an early start on the day. I went to work and it seemed that every time I left for more than a day the furniture was rearranged. Sometimes I awoke in the sleeping car on the railroad and thought "What has she done with the bedroom now?" She liked salads and I liked meat and potatoes. I liked to stay home and she wanted to go out. I liked to read and she liked TV and the movies. This may seem like a bad way to start a relationship but we both discovered that even through our loudest and most vehement arguments we always came back to each other. We argued incessantly and yelled at each other a lot, just like we were married. If anyone could consider this a courtship I must not know the meaning of the word. We had no courtship just mutual habits. I am sure that we thought we knew what we were doing but looking back I see only lonelyness and a sense of wanting to be loved and understood.

Chapter 3

Living Together

The whole time we were living together before marriage we had sex frequently. We didn't understand each other or know each others wants and likes but it somehow worked out, besides I was working as many hours as I could to pay her bills, My bills, and my ex-wife's bills so who had time to learn anything. Sex was fast and furious. Discussion about sex was infrequent and short. We never seemed to let little things like a big argument get between us and our "Play Time" as she called it. This was fine with me as I had no responsibility for her enjoyment of sex. It was entirely up to her to enjoy what we did (sensitive wasn't I.). It would take us a long time to feel comfortable enough with each other to even discuss sex and how we felt. Life for me was stressful and nerve racking. Dealing with my ex-wife, My Parents, Her parents (whom didn't like me much.), and the children. How we made it through the first few years I'll never know although she doesn't remember it that way. We continued this relationship for about another nine months before we felt (I felt) we were ready to make a commitment.

Chapter 4

The Arguments

Ah! The arguments came fast and loud. Mostly about money and the lack there of, but sometimes we would argue about jealously, my ex-wife, her ex-husband, her parents but rarely about my parents. I never knew exactly why. We were very physical people but I don't think we ever seriously came to blows in any argument. We broke a few things, slammed a few doors, stomped out of the room, and stepped out for a long drive or run, and various other standard variations on a theme. We tried to keep the children in another room while we fought (Yeah that worked). And tried to never let any of our friends or relatives see us upset. Serious discussions were still at a minimum.

Most arguments that a couple have are about money. I was no great manager of money but I will try to give my observations about money and the lack thereof. Most fights occur not because of the amount of money spent but because of unspoken expectations that couples have and are often afraid to talk about. You come home with a new "TOY" as your wife proclaims it. You paid less than half of the retail price of $500.00 but she is unhappy. Why? I'll tell you why. It's not that she didn't want you to have the toy. It's just that you have a timing issue. Maybe she sees things a little differently. She sees that she doesn't have the new things she thinks she needs. She thinks that maybe you could have consulted her before the purchase. Maybe the washer is having problems, maybe she wants ballet for your daughter, and maybe you are just stupid and unfeeling toward the needs of your family. The last of these is not true but try to convince her now and you could end up sleeping on the sofa or floor in the living room. Make an agreement that if any purchases are to be made by anyone in an amount over $100.00 that you either consult your spouse before the purchase or you sleep on it before making the purchase decision. I can remember when we were just married and I had changed careers that we didn't have much money and my wife would complain because we didn't have enough food for the children (not true) but I could eat lunch at a nice restaurant with a client or supplier. I tried to tell her that I wasn't paying for the meals (which was true) but that didn't seem to make any difference. Logic doesn't always win an argument.

Other times you will have a problem by trying to impress other people. Be it your in-laws or close friends. I know it's hard to say "We just can't afford to right now." But sometimes it may be necessary. However don't use this for every event or you may become used to using it and it becomes an excuse to not enjoy the things you can.

Another group we like to impress is our families. You figure that at Christmas you need to overspend, I mean after all who wants to be thought of as cheap at the holiday season. You can beat this by just shopping a little smarter. Begin in spring or summer to buy things for the holiday season. Sweaters and coats are marked down in spring and most styles change infrequently. Find the clearance items at the mall and buy a lot of little things instead of one or two large things. Take the time and make something homemade for someone. Some of the most cherished gifts I have were made for me by my friends and relatives. Be creative and you will look like a million bucks without spending as much.

Chapter 5

Jealousy and Religion

Jealousy has no place in any serious relationship. Great words but can anyone take them seriously? *NO!* Jealously has a proper place in any serious relationship. Who wants a mate that no one else wants. You have to feel that you are worth the person you are with or you might as well stay at home with mother.

I have seen jealously rear its ugly head. It happened at my ten year class reunion. I was there only to show all of the other people whom had made my life so miserable that I was a success. I had a good job, a sports car and a beautiful wife and children. I then ran into one of the few true friends that I had in school. I had not seen her in ten years and was very happy to see her. She was of course married and I was not interested in her in any other way than I had missed the times we had when we were young. My wife didn't seem to mind that we spent a large part of the time reliving old times but this was only skin deep. Several of the people whom wouldn't have given me their spit in high school came by and talked to me as if I had always been their best friend. Especially some of the girls who liked to make fun of me in school. Remember that when I graduated from school I was 5 foot 11 inches and 157 lbs. Now I was 6 feet 4 inches and 225 lbs. with long curly hair (not natural of course) and an undeserved attitude. When we left my wife made it plain that she was on the very verge of having a physical confrontation with some if not all of the women there. I think the words were 'They were all over you like white on rice." Not exactly what she said but I wouldn't write the exact version. I didn't see the situation like that and thought she was just a little too sensitive but I liked the thought. We didn't have a fight about it and I felt like the king of the world. I have also felt the pangs of jealousy when she went places with our friends and I didn't go, but I controlled myself. . Jealousy is only wrong when taken to the extreme. Like any other emotion taken to the extreme, danger is already there. Just like religious zeal.

Religion. I get afraid of some truly religious people because they give you a little truth with a lot of self interpretation and attitude. There is nothing wrong with being a person of faith. But when any person can see how wrong everyone else is and has the only solution then we need to be careful. When your religion becomes the encompassing thing in your life maybe you are not doing god's work but making god your work. I think that GOD placed us here to live our lives not to drop all other thoughts and think only of him. God wanted plumbers, and electricians, and doctors etc. He didn't come to monopolize man's time but to make man's time more fruitful and enjoyable by giving us a guide to live by. By showing love and compassion we are following in the footsteps of god. By helping the least of us maybe god will remember us. Is it better to build a million dollar house of god or maybe to build a smaller version and use the money to feed the hungry. God has the boundless universe to expound his glory and I think that it would be very arrogant of us to try and impress him with any sort of building, when he can build a million stars and planets with just a thought what are we to say to him "Look what we have done.". I'm not saying that we should not get together in churches and other places but the building and maintenance of a church takes up time that someone could be using to better the human condition then what is the true worth of the building. It may be hard to believe but more harm has been done in the name of religion that all of the non religious wars and plagues that have ever existed on this planet. The most dangerous person in the world is a person that is sure that they are right and everyone else must accept their truth or else. But God (believe in him or not) has always had a plan, he planned for people to be together. You can read more later about these thoughts. *You Can Believe This*. There is a soul mate out there for you. *Find them.*

Chapter 6

More Arguments and my Mother's Death

It seems that after the first year or so we were in a constant state of stress from one argument or another. Finally I decided I didn't want this anymore. Well what is one more failure in a life of disappointments? We fought for another few months and I was ready to leave and live alone on a mountain, just me and my new love, Computers. I was still working for the railroad at the time and was away in middle Tennessee. I was called by my brother and told of the situation of my mother's death. I was devestated. I drove home and arrived at my parent's home just after the county coroner left with my mother. It all happened when my father awoke that morning to discovered her lying on the kitchen floor. Calling the EMS crew he was told later that a wall in her heart had burst and even if she had been on the operating table there was nothing that could have been done. We later discovered that her heart had a weak wall from birth and no one knew. I spent the next several days sitting around with friends and relatives wondering if there was anything I could have done or said that would have made any difference. I cried when I was alone (no weakness could be shown in public). I remembered every argument we had. I to my shame wasn't even thinking of what my father was going through until the day of the funeral. I then realized that my father had lost the most important thing in his life. He had no idea how he would get through the next night much less the rest of his life. He felt that he didn't deserve her and that he had been bad to her (certainly not true). I then knew that despite all of the fights they had when I was younger, despite the accusations and the alcohol problems, despite the lack of money and education, they were soul mates. And now to see half of your soul placed in the ground was more than any person should have to bear. It was almost more than I could bear. I realized that from then on I wanted to spend more time with my father and other members of my family. It took many years for me to make all of this happen.

I know that there are a lot of computer widows out there and believe me my wife can relate. I won't presume to give you advice on this matter except to believe that this will eventually pass. It may take a few years but it should pass, mine did after I got a job as a computer and network tech at a local computer store and left the Railroad (at my wife's request). My salary dropped by more than half but my wife went back to work and wanted to help. Then the arguments started again. What else, Money. It seemed to me that she wanted to work and take the money she made and spend it as she saw fit. I on the other hand saw nothing but bills to be paid. We were both wrong there had to be a happy medium. We didn't see that at the

51

time so we argued every pay day. After the closing of the business I worked for I didn't have the slightest idea what to do. I had left a job paying $30,000+ per year for a $16,000 job that lasted less than a year. But I had my foot in the door. I studied at home and worked several volenteer jobs for free to get my name out there and then I decided that a business of my own might work. I started a small network and computer shop in our hometown. It was slow at first but it grew and so did our finances. It was quiet for about six months. Then a company whom I had delivered and Network and several computers to earlier that year called and wanted a refund after five months. I asked why and they said they had found the computers cheaper somewhere else and the software they bought (off the shelf software) didn't do what they expected. I refused stating that of course all computer hardware was cheaper five months later. That was the state of the game. Not satisfied they sued me for the cost of the computers, the software, Legal expenses, and Loss of earnings for five months. This of course placed me in bankruptcy a few months later. This was the unending source of conflict between my wife and me. I learned a lot from this experience and even if it was a bad experience it taught me something. People will do everything they can to get what they want. Even if it may seem unscruplious to someone else.

Chapter 7

My Fathers Death and My Marriage

After my mother's death I was determined to make my marriage work. I was still spending too much time with the computers but my wife seemed more understanding now and it seemed to be working out. I was hired by a company in a town twenty-five miles from home to be their network manager and programmer and the pay was at lease 2/3 of what I was making on the railroad and my wife was making up the difference. Life seemed good and I was really trying to make a life for my wife and children. Several jobs and promotions later things were only getting better.

Then in October 1985 my father passed away. This time I was able to be the strong one in the family and sort of take charge of the arrangements with my brothers and sisters. We laid our father beside my mother less than a mile from where they spent the last thirty-two years together at their home. I will not discuss how much I loved my father, but to say that my life would never be the same and from then on I tried when I made an important decision to ask myself "What would dad do". I felt that strong in the decisions my father had made with his life. He wasn't rich, especially good looking, or "Book smart", but he was probably the most intelligent man I had known in my life and I have read books by Einstein, Hawking, and Thomas Jefferson. I had finished my Bachelors degree in psychology a few years earlier and felt very smug with my education, but next to this man I was as ignorant as a young child. I am telling this to give a little more perspective on how things can happen in anyone's life. And no matter how educated we become life experience and love cannot be discounted in any situation.

Chapter 8

Conflict Resolution

This is probably the most important subject that I will discuss. At almost any point in a serious or not so serious relationship dealing with internal and external conflict will be a matter of extreme importance. How you handle any situation will decide how the next set of conditions happen. I know that all of us at one time have responded to a situation incorrectly (Duh…). And we feel bad for it later but our pride keeps us from doing anything about it. We feel that that would be a show of weakness. I know I have especially done this with my children and would never think of apologizing (more about my children later). In any adult situation this is most always the worst course of action. As with all conflict there are two sides, your side and the wrong side. I have however found out that there are probably four or more sides. Your side, the wrong side, the right side, and the side you finally decide upon. Life is a series of compromises or so it would seem. Can't get the car you want get the car you can have. Can't get the rib eye, get the hamburger. Can't get the companion you want take what you can get? WRONG!!! There are some things you have to compromise on but the most important person you will ever encounter *NEVER*. Wait and seek the one you want and work hard and you will probably find each other. I say probably because nothing in this universe is guaranteed.

Conflict begins when two people feel that one of the other is taking an unfair advantage. This may be true or it may be just a conception one or the other has. Women feel that men have all of the power and men feel that women are just waiting for the right opportunity to take full control of their lives. Neither is correct. Women want to feel that they are as important to a marriage as their husband. Husbands are trained from birth (by their mothers usually) to be the Man of the house and the breadwinner. I felt personally early in our relationship that if my wife worked I was not doing "My Job". I was as wrong about this as I could have been. My wife stayed at home with our children until they were in school. Then she went to work at night so that one of us would be with them twenty-four hours a day if necessary. I felt awful that she had to work, but imagine men what we would feel if we were told we weren't allowed to follow a career of some kind. We would feel like second class citizens. Whenever we complain about work we also feel a sense of pride at having some worth other than as someone to watch the children or mow the lawn.

Sometimes women are no better than men. Some look for the chance to not to have to work. Some want only to work in a job that has little or no actual work involved, but most women want a job that is as fulfilling and worthwhile as any man's job. That is why we have female doctors, lawyers etc. but I digress.

No matter the reason for the conflict there are a few simple questions a man should ask himself before he makes the decision to follow a conflict to its un-avoidable conclusion.

1. Are you sure you are right?
2. Are you really sure you are right?
3. Is there any way this fight will mean anything next week or next month?
4. Is there another cause of the argument that neither of you are saying anything about?
5. Could you just let it go?
6. Will this argument lead to more arguments?

Think a second before you jump in her face about whatever it is you think is so important. Remember extremely close proximity and a loud voice is not a discussion it's a fight.

Sometimes men need to argue because we feel deep down in our heart we are right, or we need to vent some anger or resentment, but try to stay as calm as possible. Not easy to do with a red faced angry female six inches from your nose trying to describe your family's lineage from the lower life forms. Somehow we always seem to say the things that we feel will do the most damage and shut the other person up. This very rarely works and can lead to feelings that are very hard to forget when the time comes for the fighting to cease and the continuation of a civil if not loving relationship to resume. Somehow "Honey you know I didn't mean all of those things I said." Just doesn't erase the memories of you calling her a female dog. Men remember, elephants don't have the memory of a woman when she is angry. She will remember every word said in anger for a minimum of 125 years. Her memory may not be accurate but if you are like most men you can't even remember your kids' birthdays so you have little or no defense against such a memory onslaught.

Women also please remember that most men are not as complicated as they may seem. Sometimes a chili dog is just as good to them as a slice of prime rib, but don't try to get them to eat spinach instead. Conflicts can be avoided by us men, sometimes very easily. There are some things that are just not important enough to fight about. Why fight when you know the outcome will be bad. Men, just let little things go and make it a point to forget it ever happened. You don't have to remember it she will. I know every man has had the experience of driving along with their wife and she seems distant or angry. You ask the fatal question. What's wrong honey? Then you may get the answer no man wants to hear. "You know what's wrong. Your stomach sinks to your shorts. You know what is coming and can see no way to avoid the pain. Then you try to remember every thing you may have done in the past six months that may have caused this situation but you draw a blank. Then you ask the fatal question. "Tell me what's wrong honey." Then you get the entire story of how last time you made this trip you did something that made her angry and she was reliving the situation and was still angry about last trip, or you may have forgotten that you promised to stop at a certain shop this time and you forgot. Or she may be remembering something you said that made her angry the other day. This is a no win situation and you will have to remind her that you are basically a simple minded slob who has a very short memory and just ask her forgiveness. Most of the time she will agree with you and let most of the anger go. This remembrance is a result of the female memory gene that allows memory storage up to and including 125 years. It may not be accurate but it does exist.

Seven Stages of any Argument

There are 7 basic stages to any argument that I see.

1. **The Anger**. This is evident when some one (usually the woman but not always) says something like "We need to talk…Right Now."

2. **The Discussion**. You are trying to make your point as calmly as possible but the other person is being unreasonable. Why can't they see you are right?

3. **The Shouting**. Not getting your point across you resort to shouting hoping the volume of your voice or your facial expression will get your point across.

4. **The Hurting**. Not being able to discuss the point in any reasonable manner you must resort to something that will get the attention of the other person and will give you the dominate position. So you try to berate and badger the other person into submission. This may include comments about their linage or lack therefore of. And their morality or lack therefore of.

5. **The Remorse**. Knowing that the argument got you nowhere and nothing was resolved you go to another room and finally think about what you have done and realize that you both said things just to hurt the other and now you feel sorry for what you said.

6. **The Rationalization**. You then rationalize your situation to place yourself in the best possible light trying to remove any guilt at what happened. After all you were right all the time.

7. **The Making Up**. If you are lucky and can swallow a little of your pride you can approach your spouse and understand that neither of you meant the things you said so you can begin again to solve the original problem. If Not the stage 6 may be as far as you can get and this will result in another argument at another time.

Resolution of any conflict is almost always the result of compromise. If compromise is not in your vocabulary please listen up. Compromise is *not* the state of giving the other person all that they want. It is the art of getting as much of what you want while making the other person believes that they are getting what they want. The truth is compromise is the state in which neither of you get all of what you want but you both get enough of what you want that you can live with the difference.

Chapter 9

Children (Yours)

Ah Children! These are the most precious people in the world (only if you are a grandparent). I have four children and I love them dearly, but sometimes I feel that all children should be placed on an island at puberty until the age of 21 then integrated into society very slowly. My children range in ages from 28 to 21. But let's return to the days of yore when all of my children were small and severely aggravating. My wife was a stay at home mom until my youngest started school. I wanted her to be there for them. I felt it important that my children have at least one of their parents available at any time and with my working out of town a lot it seemed the best solution for my wife to stay with them. I had no idea that what I was asking was practically the same as being imprisoned with three totally insane people. I discovered it when she wanted to go with a friend out of town to see a flower show and I said I would watch the children. By the time she returned the house looked like a tornado came through it and every dish in the house was dirty, and I thought I had done a good job. Nobody was dead and everybody seemed happy, except for my wife. I knew then that taking care of our children was a very difficult job. I was glad that I only had to drive railroad spikes for 40 hours per week, but let's travel on. As you know every child has his or her own personality, but my children have taken this to the extreme. I will start with my youngest daughter. When she was two years old we acquired a retired drug enforcement dog. a Doberman Pincher. After about a week we noticed that the dog didn't want to be around my daughter. I don't know what she did to this dog, and I don't believe I want to know but every time my daughter came into the room the dog wanted to go outside. Another instance happened when she was about four years of age. She was in the girl's bedroom watching a TV show when her older brother and sister came into the room sat at the foot of the twin bed and changed the channel. We heard two screams from the room and when we entered the room we saw our youngest daughter leaning back as far as she could with a handful of hair from each of the older siblings while trapping them at the end of the bed. I knew then that she would be our problem child. There were many other incidents from our children but that is a topic for another book. To say that my children were difficult was an understatement. There were constant calls from the schools and other parents. I didn't see them as anything other than being kids, but other people didn't agree. Every time a child has an argument with another child is not a case for the Supreme Court. But let's continue. We all love our children but always wish they were a bit different. We all wish that our children would love school, or maybe be more musically inclined, or had better friends. We all want our children to grow up to be famous and powerful people making a lot of money and having a happy home life. Most of the time we realize that this is almost impossible, however almost none of us want to believe that our child will grow up to be the garbage man, or the sewer worker, or a plant worker but the realization is the most people will have unspectacular jobs. This does not mean that any job must be unfulfilling. If a person loves what they do they will be the best at it. A housewife on the other hand has an enormous amount of responsibility and fear. She has to feed, bathe, clothe, and love each child individually as well as cook meals, clean house, wash cloths and mediate fights between the children. She also has to take care of another child in the family, YOU. I know we don't see ourselves as a child but we sometimes act as one. We get angry if dinner is late or we can't find our socks. We want the shiny new car, or the new wrench set, or a new fishing rod. Now don't think women don't do much the same thing but we notice it less from a woman. We expect a woman to like to shop. Men are expected to watch sports and scratch certain area of their anatomy that will not be mentioned here. Are we just stereotyping people? If the shoe fits etc. etc. etc.

Children affect a relationship in several ways. They can bring a couple closer together, Send them screaming apart, or make them ignore each other thinking that they are doing what is best for the children. And as far as I am concerned none of these are true. If you are not together in mind and emotions when the children get here it may never happen and if it doesn't it's not the children's fault.

Friction and anger between the adults is never the children's fault (unless the children are adults themselves). There is a wonderful saying that was taught to me by a Jewish friend "Children are never illegitimate only the parents have committed a sin, because the child had no part in the decision to be born." I have no patience with a man or woman who doesn't take care of their children. I have no doubt that when I was a baby that if it came to a choice of whether I ate or my parents ate I would be the one getting the food. I sometimes find this sentiment lacking in today's parents. It is always easier to think of your comfort and pleasure but when a child is present you must make sure that that child has what it needs to become all he or she can become. Love your children unconditionally and if that love is not returned don't worry. Love is never wasted, only deferred. You will be surprised how smart you will seem to your children when they have a family of their own. My children a short time from leaving home decided I was rich. They had never bought food and paid rent or auto payments and insurance not to mention utility bills. It seemed to take all of their meager resources just to survive.

Adult Children (Yours?)

The real difference between young children and adult children is the amount of money you will be shelling out. The amount asked for will change from $10 to $20 to a range from $100 to $500 or more. You probably won't mind because you are just so glad that they moved out of your house that this seems like a trivial amount (Just Kidding Kids).

Did you ever notice how repugnant it was to you when you were a young adult to think of your parents having sex? I know it sent chills of revulsion down my spine and into my stomach to even think of my parents doing the horizontal mambo in the other room. It is just as repugnant to your grown children. Some of my children say it doesn't bother them but I know better. My youngest daughter makes faces and says the "It's just wrong for old people to act like that." Sometimes my wife and I will make innuendos about sex in front of her just to get a reaction from her. After all of the embarrassment she gave us over the years this is just a little payback. Discussing sex was generally easy with my boys but it was a different thing with my daughters. I usually sent them to their mothers with intimate questions. I guess like all men my daughters will always be too young to have any intimate relationship with any male. I was lucky that my wife was always open with the children about sex and had no problem answering their questions as honestly as their maturity allowed. It was still a shock when I found a pack of condoms in the floor and confronted my sixteen year old son and he said that they weren't his. I figured that he was just embarrassed about them and I let the conversation go thinking that at least he was thinking ahead. Later that evening I discussed this with my wife and was asked what brand they were. Puzzled I asked why. She then told me that if they were a certain brand that they were not my son's but my seventeen year old daughter's. Way more information than I needed. I asked my wife franticly if my daughter was sexually active and was given the response "Certainly Not!" but my wife made it clear that if the situation arises would I feel better if she didn't have them. Now the logical answer would be "Yes I want her to be protected.", but my heart said that if I found any boy near her in any amorous situation I would pummel him until he was sure not to want anything except to escape. I made it a point that whenever a young man came to visit any of my daughters I would take his hand in a friendly handshake and squeeze until I saw him grimace with pain. Just a reminder what could happen if I became unhappy with them. Much later I found out that this daughter had sex with the man she married a few months later. However my youngest daughter didn't wait. She even told her mother when it happened. Being my rebellious daughter she found a boy she said she was in love with and wanted to marry. I thought at seventeen you are way too young to be married, besides what about school. Being herself and her mother's daughter she left school and moved in with this boy. In my state or residence there is no way I could do anything to stop them legally. They were living with his family and she ended up getting pregnant. Again the Jewish saying about children echoed in my mind. Since then they married and she gave birth to a beautiful baby girl with red hair and blue eyes who is the light of my life. They have moved out on their own and are trying to make a life for themselves. I still help financially but I really don't mind, my son's on the other hand were a slightly different matter. My oldest son quit school and married a girl when he was eighteen. She also was pregnant at the time (I didn't teach these morals in my house I hope.) She also gave birth to a baby girl who is now ten years old and very smart and pretty. It would seem that he has done alright as he graduated with his GED with high honors and wants to join the local police force. Maybe things are not so bad. My youngest son finished school and has done absolutely nothing for over four years. He sleeps at home a few nights a week. He hangs out with his friends (many of which I didn't approve of) and made just enough money to do what he wanted to do. I don't know if I was jealous or concerned but it just didn't seem right. I had worked from the time I was thirteen and could not understand him. He eventually moved out with a couple of his friends in another state. He sometimes calls and lets us know that he still loves us and when he comes by I make sure that he has a new phone card to call us with. So all in all I may not be the model parent but it just goes to prove that in spite of everything we do for our children we cannot control their destinies. We must let them be the people that they are meant to be even if we don't always approve.

Chapter 10

The Career Widow

About the time my children were in junior high I had just made a career change from building trestles and buildings for the railroad to repairing and programming computers. This was made possible by my wife agreeing to go back to work. She didn't like my other job and would do almost anything to get me to leave. It was a hard decision to give up fourteen years at the same company to virtually start over at age thirty-two. I went to work for a small computer company in my city. This meant no more traveling for a while. However I didn't know how consuming this job would be. I found myself getting immersed in the job and wanted to spend all of the time I could learning more and more about these miracles of technology. I finally bought a computer home and started to do a lot of my learning at home. I would spend hours upon hours in front of a twelve inch green screen learning as much as I could all the while neglecting my wife and children. I didn't see it that way. I was preparing for a better living for all of us (This later turned out to be true but at the time it wasn't). Six months later I was unemployed as the business went under and I was let go still being owed money. I sulked for a while and even thought of trying to go back to the railroad and beg for my job back but my wife was so confident that I would make good that it must have convinced me that maybe I had a chance after all. I decided that if I couldn't work for someone else I could work for myself. This also entailed many hours of work and effort but I kept my head above water only working seventy plus hours per week. How my marriage survived I don't know but I now feel that all of that time was not wasted. It was necessary for my success. It taught me how to be confident and how to manage money and time better. Even after eighteen years of working with computers I still have an office in my home and spend about 10-15 hours per week in there with all of my "toys". I have the luxury of doing something I love. I still do consulting for other people after my regular job, but being the best in my field I get a substantial fee for my services and am always in demand. I however limit the number of clients I have so they never interfere with my regular job. I have made a commitment to the company I work for and as long as we both hold up our agreement I will do the very best job I can for them and myself. I try to express to my children that if you are the best at what you do the money will come. You may not get rich but you will be happier. If you were wondering about the hours after work I spend in my office you should know that my wife still works at night and I usually don't spend all of my time there when she is home, at least to hear me tell it. Now that all of the children are older and we have more time and money to spend on ourselves we tend to enjoy ourselves more and more.

Now I will give my advice to the career/computer widow. FORGIVE, FORGIVE, AND FORGIVE. I know it seems that he is cold and unfeeling but remember that if he has to deal with the business world he sees only the hard cold world of finance and competition. He sees that if he doesn't do what is necessary to succeed he will always be a second fiddle or worse (if only in his eyes). And if he does what is necessary will he feel that he has done the wrong thing for the right reason. Most men gather their self image from the work that they do or the money that they make. It seems that you are never high enough on the ladder, make enough money, or have the respect of everyone you want. Your best sometimes is just not good enough. If your spouse is on a job that entails working in a sales, service or manufacturing area it can be worse because the chances for advancement are not as great and he wants to provide as much as he can for the family and gets frustrated at the knowledge that he may have to do this the rest of his life. Doing what other people say who really don't care about him or his family and would use him as a stepping stone to go just one more step up the corporate ladder if necessary. Realize this; the era of the family company is almost extinct. Corporations now look at the bottom line and will go to great extremes to make sure that the board of directors and major shareholders are happy with the profits. Most of the upper echelon have deals that would make people like us happy to get only 10% of what they earn (we usually do). The average worker in lean times are either fired or laid–off but you rarely see any corporate executives taking a reduction in pay when things go bad. A man must now walk a fine line between pleasing himself and his family and remaining employed while trying to do better for his wife and children. There are always exceptions to the rule. Some small businesses do try to make things good for their employees and most professionals (Doctors, Lawyers, and Scientists) can write their own tickets, but for the majority of the working force work is something they have to do and wish they were independently wealthy. I have nothing but sympathy for these individuals because I have been there and have felt the same way. This is just an over simplification of what I believe is happening to the American worker. In my own way I wanted to try to explain to the woman of the house how a man can get his identity by what he does and why it is important for a man or a woman to have the support and understanding of a spouse. Inspiring a spouse is not hard. Just tell them "They can accomplish anything they set their mind and soul to." And believe it yourself. Remember also that no person will consider themselves successful unless they have the respect and admiration of their mate. The old saying of "You are what you do.", Was never truer.

Chapter 11

Priorities

The priorities of a young family are not necessarily the priorities of an older more mature family. Why do I speak as if a family is a child growing up to adulthood? Because for a fact the family is. It is a living breathing entity sanctioned by the creator for humanity. We have to feed it, nurture it, and help it grow until it has learned to help take care of itself. A family starts usually with two people who are offshoots of other families. It then grows by making more offshoots and sheltering them as they grow, then it gets older and the offshoots go on their way to grow more families, hopefully happy and healthy individuals making a contribution to the world. The family is then fully mature with many offshoots and a mature structure at its base to give it stability and protection from the elements. Then finally the base of the old tree will die and leave a lasting impression on the earth for the latest offshoots to hopefully learn from if the family has a sound foundation to begin with. There are many variations on this theme but this is how I see it.

When my wife and I were first together some of our priorities were to have a good time and try to get back at the people whom we saw as the protagonists of our lives if only in our minds.. We would sit for hours and discuss how we would get these people and how wrong these people were to try and interfere with our lives. We never really intended to do any of these things but it let us vent the anger. We would ignore our parents because they were not really of any use to us, but we still loved them as long as they didn't try to change us or convince us we were wrong. Money was scarce so we satisfied ourselves with work, sex and exercise not necessarily in that order. We would save money to go to clubs, dinner and movies even though we couldn't afford it. We drank too much when we drank (very very rarely) and talked our enemies down as much as possible. We were self centered, self superior, and all in all very selfish, but we figured with all we had been through we were worth it. We fought frequently knowing for certain that the other person was invariably wrong to the core. We had sex just for the sake of having sex or maybe just to loose ourselves from the daily grind of having to put up with other people and each other. We exercised just so other people could see how in shape and happy we were. We went out with what we called friends just to show that we were as cool as anybody else. It was a very strange and lonesome existence. It was also very childish of us. I am sure that most of the people we knew at the time were in somewhat the same boat as us even if they won't admit it. It took the death of my mother to change the situation and for me to re-evaluate my priorities. It wasn't that I ignored my mother. I visited as much as possible and never missed a chance to giver her (or my father for that case) a hug or a kiss. I guess I just felt that I had outgrown that part of my life to an extent. It was a great shock when she passed away very unexpectedly at the age of sixty-three.

Chapter 12

The Right Priorities?

As I spent more time with my father I learned a lot about how to deal with life. He said "It sometimes takes a loss to let you know what you still have." I gained more respect for my father after my mother left than I had ever had before. I saw strength in him that I could only hope to emulate. Now to my _New_ priorities. As I have learned from all of this self introspective I am not the center of the universe. It brings to mind the quote from the Wizard of OZ: "Remember you are not judged by how much you love, but by how much you are loved by others". I realized then that I was a very rich man whether I knew it or not. I had the love of my father and my wife and if that wasn't enough I had the love of a small brown eyed girl who thought I could deliver the moon if she wanted it bad enough. I figured I had the love of my four brothers and sisters but I felt it was another kind of love. To them I would always be the baby brother who needed to be guided by them. I knew then that if I was going to do anything that would bring me satisfaction I was going to have to make a few sacrifices and work very hard at my profession and my relationships. My wife was going to be a major part of my life and there was no way I was going to fail. I have made it a practice to take some time on a regular basis to just sit and re-evaluate my priorities. If you believe your priorities won't change at different stages in your life your are wrong. It usually takes a catastrophic incident to make us think but sometimes something seemingly unimportant will make you think. The situation that I remember was when I was in my middle twenties and was told that a friend that I knew well from school was killed in an automobile accident just a short distance from my home. I remember driving by this particular acccident and remembered that I felt almost nothing when I passed. After finding out that it was someone I considered a friend my mortality came into question and fear set in.

Chapter 13

You and your Spouse After 40

There is nothing magic about the number fourty unless you are a woman. The number thirty seemed to be a more traumatic number than fourty to my wife but I digress. Things somehow change after fourty. You tire easier; your sex drive has driven off (to some extent). Everything you eat either goes to your stomach ,hips or to gas. You find sleep more attractive than Jay Leno. You catch yourself watching the news channels, for hours. The songs you listen to are considered beyond oldies. No one remembers who Spiro Agnew was. And so forth. But in a lot of cases the marriage relationship gets better. The children are grown or almost grown. The house is yours again. You have to a certain extent more expendable cash and time to spend it. This is a good time to plan more excursions for you and your spouse. I know what most of you men are thinking, There goes Monday night Football, but Oh Contraire!. Your spouse needs more of you now than ever even if she hasn't said anything. She is probably in a routine with you that includes not speaking to you during baseball or football season. Getting grunts instead of responses to questions while you are watching TV or reading a book in bed while you watch Leno. But think. You can have more fun than you ever thought you could and have to give up almost nothing. Let's look at a few instances where you can do something unexpected. Here is a small list.

1. When she asks you to bring home food for dinner call ahead to a stylish restaurant and get dinner instead of KFC or McDonalds. Go all the way, Salad, Bread, and Steak or Seafood and maybe desert and server it to her.

2. Bring her flowers for no reason (you only have to stop at almost any grocery store)

3. If the Ballgame is a blowout ask her to go get an ice-cream with you and talk.

4. Buy or even print on your computer greeting card saying something nice about her.

5. Surprise her with a get away to a hotel with a hot tub or spa if only for one night.

6. Take her to the Zoo and just walk around.

7. If you have a convertible or can borrow one take her on a ride late in the summer evening and just talk about nothing. Have soothing music to listen to.

8. Give her the Cinderella re-wedding. You can spend a little or a lot but the sentiment will be there with the knowledge that she has that you would do the same thing over again only

trying to do it better. Invite all of her friends and relatives and plan a small honeymoon for after.

9. Cuddle with her while watching a movie on TV and have some of your favorite wine and cheese handy, or beer and Chips as you prefer.

10. Have sex on the sofa for a change. (or anywhere different)

11. Be sure to hold your spouse after sex. A cuddle or kiss means so much more after sex than during. You don't have to spend hours holding or talking but don't just roll over and go to sleep and for heaven's sake don't turn the TV back on just to see Leno five minutes after you finish. This time is usually a good time to talk about your feelings and wants and what you can do to make sex more enjoyable for the both of you.

There are many more that you could try. You should know by now what your spouse likes, if not try asking. You might be surprised what you will learn. Most of all talk to her. You might be surprised at how much you both have in common and how you share the same opinions on a lot of things. If you however find that you seem to have less in common then you did in earlier years, this is still not a huge problem. Everyone likes something nice done for them from time to time. It will pay many dividends in return and the more you do the easier it gets.

From most of this chapter you have heard me preach to the men. Now for the women of the house. It may be true that women are more emotional than men but men still have feelings. That slug on your sofa watching the baseball game in his underwear is not unfeeling. He has been taught from birth to be the strong member of the family. No matter how you tell him that crying at a movie doesn't make him less of a man he probably won't break into tears watching the movie "Steel Magnolias". Maybe we men lack an imagination or maybe we just don't get the emotional feelings watching movies. To us I think it must be a little more personal. Men feel the same emotions women do but maybe not in the same way. Example: a neighborhood dog is hit by an automobile and is dying. A woman may cry and try to help the dog, while a man may want to hurry up and help the dog die knowing that nothing can be done for the animal. To the woman this seems cruel and callous, but the man just cannot bear to see any animal suffer when there is a solution, Same Emotion "Pity", different reaction. A man may sometimes see a movie and think "Boring!!!" while a woman finds the same movie very "Emotional" or "Sensitive". Just different sides of the same coin flipped. Now for things a woman can do that are easy and will probably make the man feel like a contented puppy.

1. Don't ever trivialize a man's work or serious interests. I know women to think that anything a man does that he enjoys must be playing. Not like Playing Golf, Like asking "Why do you play with that computer so much?" or "Are you going to Play with that Car again today?" How would you like it if your man said "Are you going to play with the dishwasher all day?" Sounds stupid doesn't it. Men tend to take their hobbies and other interests very seriously even though most other people don't.

2. Don't be indecisive. When a man asks you where you want to go for dinner please for pity sake don't say "I don't care" unless you really don't care. Nothing makes a man more uncomfortable and irritable than to choose a restaurant and you say "I don't want to eat there." A man appreciates a woman who says instead "I think I would like some Chinese" or 'I think I would like some baked chicken". These at least give us an option and a direction for us to go. Men don't like making all of the decisions.

3. Never criticize his parents. Even if his parents are axe murderers you will accomplish nothing by berating any member of his family. He may do it but you shouldn't. Remember you didn't have to live with these people and should try not to make judgments about them. I am sure that you feel the same way about your family. If not, I'm sorry for you.

4. Don't deny Sex / Love out of anger. I don't mean that after you have an argument that you should just jump into the sack like rabbits on Noah's Arc, but don't deny yourself and your spouse the pleasures that come from intimacy because you feel that it would give you an advantage. The advantage is short lived and may cause more harm than good. I know women think that a man when it comes to sex a man is just like a dog with no feelings except in his groin, but this is not necessarily true. Any woman who uses sex to control a husband only has control until the man finds a new sex

partner. If you treat sex like a reward for a puppy, the puppy will find another bitch to help relieve the tension. And why would you deny yourself the pleasure. There is an old saying. "Love missed is gone forever." If you miss a chance to get or give pleasure the chance for that opportunity is gone forever. You may make love a thousand more times but you will have missed this particular opportunity.

5. Try to build your spouse. A huge task, especially after fourty. Something happens to a man when he reaches a certain age. It doesn't happen to all men but it happens to most. We feel that our heyday is gone. We feel that the only way to be attractive to other women (Not for Sex or love but for admiration and respect) is to do something spectacular. This is sometimes called 'The Mid-Life Crisis". Some men divorce their wives and get a younger wife (Which almost always ends in failure) or buys a new expensive sports car (See what I can afford) or tries to have sex at the drop of a hat…any hat. Men are strange creatures when we feel inadequate. We stress out and get belligerent. Unlike the menopause in women there seems to be no reason for these changes but believe me they are real. A man must feel that he is the superior mate for this woman or he is of no use to anyone. In these situations a man may spend a great amount of time at work to show that he is an important part of the company he works for. He may also try to avoid any intimate settings that may lead to sex for the fear that he will be judged as lacking in the sex

department. He may pick a fight to prevent any chance of you wanting sex. Or the opposite may be true. He may loose all interest in things that seemed important to him just a few years earlier. He may become demanding of you in the sex department just to prove to that he hasn't lost anything in the past twenty or so years. Neither is a good situation for you or for him. The best thing is to talk to him. He probably won't be co-operative but he will eventually talk to you if he feels that you are seriously interested and not just wanting information to complain to your friends about his problems. Find a time when he is relaxed or in a good mood. Don't be forceful but be frank. Don't say "What the hell is wrong with you?" rather say "Honey, I've noticed a few changes in you can we talk about them." He may not be ready then but now he knows you are interested. Don't press the matter but be ready to broach the subject again at the opportune time. Then be supportive and let him know what a good provider and father he has been. Let him know that he is still the man you want and need. This seems simple but it will work wonders.

6. Don't take advice from any woman's magazine or single friends. These may be fine for the latest recipe but not for your marriage. You will be just asking for trouble. If you feel you need advise check with someone you know is happy in their relationship, not someone who gets paid ten cents per word to fill a page, or has stayed single for fourty years. Just because someone is a doctor or has a degree , or "Has

her own life." doesn't make them any better at relationships. Doctors have a greater rate of divorce than the national average. If they are so smart why can't they save their own relationships? And just why is your friend single? Do they have trouble committing to a relationship?

You will notice that the advice that I gave the women is basically what not to do. You may think that I am critical of women but the real reason is that women already do most of the things that make a man feel comfortable and wanted. You cook his meals. Clean his cloths, do most of the child rearing, and provide sex and intimacy for him. As long as you are not a total badgering, critical, of self-centered woman you are probably doing just about everything you can to make the relationship work, but only you and your spouse can make that determination.

Men, remember to tell your wife often how much she means to you. If you cannot tell her in words tell her with deeds. "A single kiss with love means more than a thousand roses with indifference". Nice quote huh.

Chapter 14

Your love life after 40

The saying "Life Begins at fourty" was written by a person who was either single or delusional or both. After fourty life generally is trying to beat you across the head with a big stick". Your body doesn't work like it did only a few years ago. The male libido is diminished somewhat. Sex is probably not the most important thing to achieve daily, and the job is becoming a tedious task. But have hope. Love is still there in a greater amount than you know. I have the idea the most younger people (Younger than thirty) think love is the act of having sex as much as possible and as long as possible with someone that you are attracted to. I feel that true love is not the young woman you wake up to after a few months of marriage but the woman you awaken with after many years of marriage and you still want to have her by your side for the rest of your life. I have a lot of trouble just telling my wife "I Love You." I think that these words fall from the lips too easily. How may young men tell women that they love them when they don't mean it? Or it may become a habit for you to tell your wife 'I love you' before leaving for the day as a reflex. Women like to hear these words and men say them without meaning. It never hurts to say the words but never think that fulfills the obligation you have. There are other ways that you can show the feelings. When she walks by reach out and taker her hand, she will probably slow down before releasing your hand but you made the effort to touch her without any obligation of a response from her. When you see her doing dishes come from behind her and give her a small hug and soft kiss on her neck or ear. You may be surprised by the response. Always make her feel that these things do not necessarily require a response. You are just acknowledging her existence and value to you. You should be able to find a million other ways to say what you feel without very much effort. These things will become second nature to you and you will feel strange when she is not around for you to do them.

I will now approach the subject of a sexual life after fourty. Really there is no difference in the sex life from year thirty-nine to fourty. Fourty is no magic number. But you will start to notice a few problems with you urge around this time. Whether it is due to a physical or psychological reason a male sex drive will diminish. You find that climax may happen a little faster or you may have a harder time getting in the mood. This doesn't mean that you enjoy sex less. It just means that you have had sex for a lot of years and you know just about what you expect and some of the excitement may be lacking. Hope arises eternal. You need to discuss this with your spouse. I had a really hard time talking to my wife about what

I liked and we were married for twenty years. It became easier when I discovered she truly wanted to know what I liked and wanted. We are children of the seventies and felt we were enlightened about sex and knew all we needed to know. How far from the truth can two people get? Sure we had orgasms, usually not at the same time but we had them. We felt great and relaxed but sometimes I felt a little unfulfilled. I am sure she did also but we never mentioned it to each other. I still find it hard to tell my wife what I would like, but most times I get the information across to her. Some women feel that sex is something required of them and if they enjoy it too much something is wrong with them. Two thousand years of religious training cannot be forgotten in just a few decades. I have always felt that if a woman does not enjoy sex with her partner after a few years of marriage that the husband is *usually* to blame. No Man Bashing Here just Facts. Women I have found have more serious hang-ups about the kind of sex that they want. They feel that if they want anything except standard penis/vagina copulation that there is something wrong with them. This comes from when our forefathers were so afraid of being seen as immoral or not religious that everything that was not seen as standard was considered evil or deviant. I also feel that any sexual act done by two consenting adults should only be the business of the people involved. As long as no one is harmed why should any other person judge the correctness of your actions? If god doesn't see fit to interfere why should anyone else try?   Women of the past and even in my generation were taught that oral sex was plain bad and nasty. I have always been puzzled as to why most men like giving and getting oral sex and women seem to be on the receiving end only as a matter of correctness. They were taught for centuries that sex was only for the creation of children. This is still taught today in several 3rd world countries where it is considered a sin for women to enjoy sex. I also feel that what a couple does in private should never be discussed with friends or relatives unless advice is asked and never with strangers. Please remember that most men have dreams of oral sex and a lot of women find the prospect repugnant. If you feel this way please let your spouse know and don't give up until you have made the assessment for yourself. I am not pushing any sexual act you would not be comfortable with but don't be afraid to experiment and let your partner know if you just don't want to do something. Men remember "Sex is like a Chinese dinner. The meal is not through until everyone has their cookies." Never leave your spouse hanging unless there is no other option. There is more than one way to make a cake.

Don't get me wrong I know that there are some acts of sex that are deviant. . In my opinion sex with children is deviant and must be punished as well as forced sex either through physical force or coercion. I know that we men have dreams of having sex with more than one woman at a time but most women would not like to share their spouse and most men feel the same way. I guess the dream comes from the reaches of the male brain to have totally meaningless sex with complete strangers without the entanglements of a serious relationship. I have had these thoughts and don't really know where they come from. There is nothing wrong with a fantasy life as long as you are smart enough to know that you should never act upon these urges. In many ways you must have a strong imagination if you want to make your sex life with your spouse as much fun and exciteing as you possibly can. There is that key word again FUN. Sex should be fun and fulfilling. If not then there is some serious talking to be done and men, you must keep an open mind as much as the women.

Chapter 15

Why your children don't understand your sexuality

When my children became teenagers their attitudes changed (DUH!) The were becoming sexual beings and I felt that it was my responsibility to make it as hard as I possiblly could for them to find any opportunity to do anything sexual with anyone else. I was correct in protecting them but they didn't seem to know why I was doing what I was doing. They thought I was interfering in their lives, and I was. Even thought they did not appreciate the effort I was making I continued to try (repete the word try) to quote "Interfere" with any exploration of the sexual world. About the time they were doing the experimentation without my knowledge they realized that their parents were still sexually active and were totally disgusted. They figured that we had given up sex when they were born. Having our bedroom on the other end of the house they never heard any noises and as our door locks we had Very few surprise visits when we were occupied. The main reason that your children don't want to think about you and sex in the same sentence is obvious. Just think of your parents in an undressed and undignified position with your mother shouting "Ride me like a wild pony cowboy", and you will get a slight understanding of their position. You will just have to live with the thought that no matter how they say that it doesn't bother them to think of you and sex "THEY ARE LYING". If you want to have some fun while the children are visiting just toss around a few sexual innuendos and watch your children squirm. Even though we have fewer sexual hang ups than our parents and it seems that the younger generation have even fewer we are still a long way from total sexual freedom (Thank God). If we remove all of the mystery and secretive things from sex it will be just another thing we do for fun like going to a movie or eating out at a casual restaurant. Everyone loves to do something that they know they shouldn't do and some of the excitement from sex may come from the heightened awareness that you may be discovered at any time. Even our children whom we think are never ready for sex will try to sneak around when they think you don't know what they are doing. The best thing may be to do what our parents have done for the last 2000 years. Don't discuss your sex life with your children. I am not saying not to discuss sex and the consequences of sex with your children, but stay away from specifics. Let them have the fun of finding out for themselves.

Larry L. Hall Sr. Ph.D

Why we don't understand our own sexuality

I would estimate that about 80% of us don't understand our own sexuality. No matter how much we want to we run up against the wall of fear and misunderstanding. I was not raised by a puritan family; however my parents never discussed sex and or a sexual relationship with me. I felt that sex was a subject that polite people didn't discuss. I was extremely curious to a state of being consumed with the subject but I was sure to let no one know as I felt that this was evil and therefore made me a bad person. All of my brothers and sisters were married before I was ten or so but I never related them with any kind of sexual relationship. I went the rout of any pre-teen boy and sneaked a look at pornographic books that I found. Maybe not the best way to learn but at that time options were limited. An incident that happened to me just reinforced the concept that I was bad when at the age of twelve in our class brought some books to school. Several of us were sneaking a look at these books when a teacher noticed what we were doing. The five of us were immediately marched to the principal's office and were lectured to about the evils of what we were doing. I think the most damaging thing said to me was "If you fill your head with this kind of garbage then you are no better than the garbage you look at." This was worse than the ten licks (Swipes with a wooden paddle that to me looked like a sawed off baseball bat) we were given by the P.E. Coach as punishment. I feel that this may have harmed me more than anything up until this time. I was convinced that nude women and sex must have been the

92

most evil thing a man could think of and that my worth as a human must be diminished by what I was thinking and looking at. The fact that I just went further underground with my thoughts made me feel even lower. I was in my twenties before I could loose most of this feeling and even today at fifty-one I still have trouble not thinking of myself as some sort of sexually deviant person although in my heart I know differently. I am sure that the people in the school thought they were protecting me from some evil but to this day I have a hard time with a school that teaches in history class that it is fine to fight and kill when told to do so for a cause but don't even think of having sex just for fun or mutual satisfaction. Don't get me wrong, there are a lot of times that sex is inappropriate and just in plain bad taste, but I can see very few cases when the act of sex between two consenting adults should be the concern of anyone else including our government. Now that you see maybe why I have had a time relating to sex let me go a little further. I have done many things in my life that I am ashamed of as has everyone else. I have done things that I knew was wrong but always have regretted them later. However I have not in the past twenty years or so had any sex that I have regretted. I have enjoyed sex probably the most in the past ten years. I know that I have been married for twenty-four years and the sex was always good but for the last ten years my wife an I have discussed all aspects of us and we have discovered that most married coupled will discuss their sex lives with almost any friend but will keep silent with their partners. This is a shame, for who can tell you what she likes better that her. I know that it is hard to talk to your partner. Nothing could be worse that to tell your partner what you would like just to have them make a disjointed face or worse to say something like "What would make you think I would even think of something like that." I have discussed this with my wife and have made an assumption that she seems to agree with. Women can drive a man to have sex with someone else just by not enjoying sex. Let me explain. I have always been under the impression that if a woman is not enjoying sex with her husband then her husband is not giving a full effort to accomplishing his goal. I have heard that some women just want the man to hurry and finish so it will be over and I know some men just don't care and would just as soon hump and sleep. I feel nothing but pity for these people. Although a quickie can be fun and stimulating hurrying sex just to finish is a waste of everybody's time and effort. Some women never have an orgasm while having normal (What is normal?) sex, but there are other ways of bringing pleasure to your spouse. Having an orgasm without penal penetration is not a sin. This works both ways. If a man wants a certain kind of sex and his wife is adamant that this will never happen try something else. If your wife is reluctant about oral sex as most women were trained to be don't be demanding. If you treat her the way she needs to be treated you may be surprised how far she may go to try to make you happy. I always felt as a younger man that oral sex was degrading for the female but this is not so. It may not be the most favored of women but when they find out how much pleasure most men get from this it will become if nothing else not so much a chore. Men remember that the woman is doing this because she loves and trusts you, most women don't get a lot of pleasure having something pushed in her face so be gentle. And also remember that she deserves only your best effort in making sex pleasurable for her. As was stated in a movie I was watching late one night *"Sex is like a Chinese dinner. It isn't over until you both get your cookies."* I just had to use this quote again. Most of all enjoy each other. If it is the wrong time of the month for her maybe you should just try to hold her before you go to sleep. If you think that intimacy is only achieved by having sex then you are missing 50% of the time you could be enjoying with your spouse. Intimacy is not a touchy feely word it is a state of mind. In conclusion the reason we don't understand our own sexuality is because we are afraid. Afraid that our spouse will make us feel inadequate, deviant, perverted, unloved or just make sport of our fantasies and sexual preferences. Afraid that our friends may laugh and make light of our sensitivity, and that we just don't make the grade as a good mate for your spouse. Afraid that our weakness for sex will be used against us by someone we love. Sex is not a weakness, it is a gift from a loving god to be used between two people who care about each other and want to give and get pleasure. For all of those people who say sex is just for procreation I say that a female is only fertile about 10% of any given month but sex was made available from god anytime we want it. What a loving god we must have to give us that much opportunity for love and gratification.

Chapter 17

RE-Marriage

When I say re-marriage I don't mean after a divorce. After many years of living with my wife I found myself looking for ways to show how much she means to me. I am not the kind of man that say's "I Love You" often though I should. I feel that if I have to say it all of the time I may be trying to convince myself that it's true, so much for confidence. We had been together for twenty-one years. Things were going well for us and we were secure in our relationship. I decided that a surprise wedding would be in order. We were originally married in a small town in Georgia called Ringgold. We were married by the justice of the piece. I borrowed $50.00 to buy the license and blood tests and gave the JP $15.00 for the ceremony. Having to give an out of state address or wait three days I gave my address as 1600 Pennsylvania Ave. Washington DC. No questions were asked and no explanations were given. For several years after I tried to convince my wife that we really weren't married as I had lied on the license but she wasn't biting. But I digress. I had planned

All That I Am Is Here

to give my spouse the Cinderella wedding that she had missed. Plans were being made. I researched many places and decided on a small chapel in the Smoky Mountains just outside of Gatlinburg Tennessee. I wanted to go all the way and had set aside what I considered a small fortune just for this adventure. I contacted a local shop about bridal gowns and searched the city for dresses. Being as I have no taste in clothing (as anyone can tell you) I requested the services of my oldest daughter. We searched for several hours and then stumbled upon this little shop on the outskirts of town. I found what I thought was the most beautiful gown I had ever seen. Now the problems arose. What size dress did my wife wear? Being a man and ignorant in such things I discovered that most wedding gowns had to be custom fitted. I decided that I would figure out that problem later so I paid for the gown and accessories such as a veil, undergarment support, and was told that I would need a pair of white shoes and pantyhose. Now I needed Tuxedos and Dresses for the others in the party. I called each son and made it clear that I expected everyone to be present at this function. Not being there would negate anything they expected in my will (just kidding). I knew that keeping a secret like this for three months was going to be a feat comparable to the D Day Invasion of Normandy. I made sure that the dress shop did not have my home address or phone number so no calls would be forthcoming. Now I wanted my two daughters to wear the same color dress that my wife had been married in, not knowing Peach was not a popular color in this day and age which means I had to find a dress maker to custom make the dresses for them. This took three weeks and many calls. While making arrangements for the Tuxedos I found a small size 4T tuxedo in the store and thought that my grandson would look adorable in tails so I purchased it as it was not for rent. The other four including mine were to be delivered a week before the wedding date and we were to come and be fitted a week prior to the delivery date. The dresses were to be ready two weeks prior to the date of the wedding. Also in another dress store I found a dress for my granddaughter that mimicked my wife's wedding gown and purchased it for her. Now the problems started. six weeks before the wedding my oldest son was making excuses not to bring our granddaughter around to visit and my wife was getting very ill. When I talked to him privately later he said that all my granddaughter could talk about was the dress and the upcoming wedding so he didn't dare bring her around. I later explained to my wife that my son and his wife were having problems and just needed some time to work them out so we should just leave them alone for a few weeks. She was still angry but agreed to wait to jump them. Now the problem was to get my wife sized for the gown. I finally came up with a plan. Earlier I had purchased two tickets to the Fox Theatre in Atlanta for the Phantom of The Opera. We were just going to go down and return the same night. I then convinced her that we should do something special for this occasion and maybe stay the night and dress up as we almost never have an occasion to get dressed up for anything. I told her I would make reservations for the Polaris Restaurant and we would make a night of it. I knew that she didn't have anything to wear even with a closet full of cloths so I took the opportunity to go shopping with her and we found this little dress shop on the outskirts of town. How fortunate. She was then measured up and down and she finally decided on two gowns that she liked a long Golden Yellow dress and a Long Lavender gown. Purchasing these two gowns and letting the dress shop measure her I was now ready for the wedding, or so I thought. My wife then decided that I needed a new suit. So off to the mall we went and purchased two new suits. By now this is getting expensive. The closer to the wedding the more nervous I got. I had made reservations at a hotel in Gatlinburg for the other members of the family fourteen to be exact including her mother and grandmother. I had reservations at a nice restaurant for the reception as well as the limousine and wedding cake. Most of these arrangements were made by the chapel including the honeymoon suite and champagne for the room. I then decided she needed a new ring as when we were married she used a sapphire ring turned around so the stone didn't show as a wedding ring. I went shopping and decided on a regular gold band but I wanted something special for a new engagement ring. Over the years I had bought my wife many diamonds and other jewelry but I wanted this to be simple and special. I found what I was looking for at a local shop. It was a Heart shaped diamond ring. Not a large stone but very pretty. It would be ready a week before the trip. I was now ready. Yea Right. Still almost a month away I approached my wife and as I am likely to do once or twice a year I announced that we were going to take a long weekend in Gatlinburg in the middle of July. I expressed that we would go alone and not be bothered by anyone or anything for three days and we needed the break. She then gave me a scare when she said 'You know the kids will want to do something for your birthday that week so we might as well stay home and wait." I said that going to the Smokies was what I wanted for my birthday and she acquiesced to my request. She then got a little excited and for the next few weeks all she could talk about was how we were going to be alone and enjoy the trip with no children, grandchildren or other family to bother us. I was starting to be apprehensive about the whole thing. The week of the wedding arrives. We were to leave Thursday morning and return Saturday night. Tuesday I picked up the wedding Gown and Tuxedos. My daughter was to pick up the custom made dresses the same day (Two weeks late). I had the dresses and tuxes hanging in my office with a notice in the front that I was to be called if my wife came by for any reason. Being a former musician for the last six weeks I had been writing and trying to record a special song for the wedding. I had to do my recording late at night while my wife was at work and it only took fourty-three takes to get something that I thought I would not be totally ashamed of. I had arranged for the chapel to use my music for some of the video being taken of the wedding. Finally the day came. I awoke early from a not so sound sleep. I couldn't help but think that she already knew everything and was just playing around with me. We were going to take the convertible that I had been restoring for several months so for sure it looked like rain. I had my cell phone and a long distance phone card so I could keep in touch with the entourage that was to follow us to our destination, so we lost touch immediately. I decided to take the long and scenic way around and they decide to take the interstate. On the way we stopped at a location that I thought was romantic. A place where a small dam was releasing water for whitewater rafters and kayakers. We sat on a rock with a watery mist around us and I casually asker her if she would do it again. 'Do what again?" she said. "Marry me." I said. She replied "Of course I would." I then gave her the new heart shaped diamond ring. It was dwarfed by the ring she already had on her finger but you would have thought that I had given her the Hope diamond. I might have also mentioned that the surprises were not over for this day but left her hanging. We drove on with then top down until it really started to rain. We laughed and pulled the top up and continued on. Later that morning the rain lifted and we dropped the top before we got to the mountains. The Mountain Laurel was in full bloom and the smell was heavenly as we went across the mountain to Gatlinburg from Cherokee . We arrived about two hours ahead of schedule, I finally contacted my daughter via cell phone and was told that the hotel could not find our reservation confirmation and I would need to stop by and give them my credit card information. As we were talking however they found the information and all would be fine. As we were going through town so that I would have an idea of where the chapel was I noticed my daughter-in -law's van coming up on the left. I had to quickly distract my wife. I asked her where we were and would she look on the map and help me find the hotel we were staying at. She was so intent on the map that she missed them completely. Being two hours ahead of time I was concerned. I finally decided to go and see the people at the chapel. I parked about a half block away from their office and told my wife that I would be right back. I wanted to see if we could check in early. I went into the office and identified myself and asked if I could get the key to our suite. They were more than helpful and asked if someone could go over and remove the champagne and other items that might give the surprise away. I told them I would take care of it myself. Having the key and directions to the suite we departed. Getting to the room I asker her if she would please check in the trunk for my camera so I could take some pictures outside the suite. Knowing that my camera was on the bottom gave me some time to get inside and hide some of the things. After that I went and helped her find my camera and carried the luggage into the room. She was very happy with the room. It had a fireplace (not very useful in July) and a heart shaped whirlpool tub in the middle of the room. We had a view of a small stream off of the rear deck and there were rose pedals on the bed. She was somewhat tired and wanted to freshen her makeup. I told her to relax that our dinner reservations were not until 7:00 PM. this was at 4:30PM. When about 5:30 came I figured it was time to leave. We got into the car and headed out. I intentionally drove past the chapel twice hoping that our children would get there first. However when I pulled up at 5:50PM another wedding was just finishing up and my wife said the six words that will send chills up my spine. "I have to go to the Bathroom." I tried to convincer here that this was not the place to need a pit stop but she would not be dissuaded. She went up the small hill to the chapel with me in tow and asked to use the facilities. While she stepped into the restroom I was panicky. No dress, no tuxedos, and no children. I spoke to the people and they were ready. I then walked outside expecting to commit suicide when lo and behold two vans appeared in the distance. It was the entourage with all of the necessities in tow. I immediately grabbed my tux and went into the groom's dressing room. I heard my daughter say to my wife "Come on we got to Hurry." I was dressed and came out of the dressing room while the minister was briefing everyone on their parts. I was escorted down the isle with my oldest son as my best man. We waited about five minutes when the music started. My youngest son escorted his mother down the isle and I swear she looked even more beautiful that the day we married. The ceremony was very tasteful and seemed to last for a long time, but how do I judge time at a moment such as this. We both repeated our vows to each other and kissed. It was as the first time except neither of us was embarrassed to kiss in front of the people there. We were then taken into another room where we were sent back into the chapel and introduced to everyone there as Mr. and Mrs. Larry L. Hall. This was the opportunity for the photographer and videographer to work their magic. We were then led outside where the next surprise was waiting. Waiting outside was a Stretch white limousine and chauffeur waiting to take us around town and back to our suite. We were driven around the center of town a couple of times which took about an hour, all the time we were chattering like a couple of teenagers on a first date. When we arrived at out suite we went in and changed cloths. The reception was scheduled for 7:00PM at a restaurant a couple of blocks away. We were the first to arrive and I checked and everything was as planned. We had a private dinning room and the wedding cake was there. We waited at the bar for everyone else to arrive and I started a tab for everyone. We then proceeded to the area and had a wonderful dinner and cut the cake saving the top layer for our next anniversary. When we returned to the room I broke out the champagne and chocolate and some special music I had brought for us and we enjoyed the whirlpool tub together. We didn't have sex that night but neither of us seemed to mind, probably because we were just physically and emotionally drained from the day.

Just to show that even dream occasions sometimes have pitfalls the next day we left to site-see and I picked up the wrong set of keys. These keys did not have a room key on them. When we returned at about 10:00PM that evening and we couldn't get into our suite. My wife made the comment that she wouldn't mind if we had to sleep in the car with the top down and watch the stars if necessary but I didn't agree. The business office was closed and I was getting a little stressed. Finally we drove up to the chapel and the minister had another set of keys to the suite. I commented that if nothing else happened that we were very lucky. The rest of the trip was very restful and the drive home wonderful. I plan to live off of the glory of this event for at least another ten years if not longer.

Chapter 18

Surprises

Not everyone loves a surprise, at least that's what they say. But how many of use would hate to find a $20 bill in the pocket of out coat we haven't worn since last winter. Or to find that we are the winner of the lottery. In this line of reasoning you must realize that most of us like a pleasant surprise. However there are surprises that no one wants or needs. Like finding out that your car needs a new engine or that your wife is only staying with you because you make a good living. But I don't want to drag this discussion into the depths of despair. I want to talk of all of the small and pleasant surprises that you can do for each other that will make you feel better and do a world of good for your relationship. First of all don't try to impress your spouse with a lot of expensive presents. This may backfire as it may arouse suspicions that are not founded and most people just cannot afford it. Second do not surprise your spouse too often or this will make the surprises either expected or make the expression mean less. Third do be generous without being extravagant, I remember that I was returning from an overnight trip when I stopped at a farmer's market to get some fruit. I noticed that they had a special on roses 2 ½ dozen for….Well lets say about ¼ the normal amount, as my anniversary was approaching I seized the opportunity and bought 7 ½ dozen of these flowers. I made quite and impression for a relatively small amount of money and a little effort. But I try to make it a point to do something on a pretty regular basis. I mean how much trouble is it on the way home from work to stop by a grocery store and buy a couple of dollars worth of flowers for your wife. But don't just bring them home hand them to your wife and ask what's for dinner. Take a few seconds and make sure she knows that you did this because she is the one you love and glad she is there. This is probably the simplest and least expensive of the things I can suggest. However this is not the only thing possible. It largely relies on personal taste. Other women may like other things better, like small chocolates, or her favorite ice-cream, or a special wine she appreciates. The list is endless. However once in a while do something spectacular. I said spectacular not expensive. Like plan an evening for her without her knowledge. Have an overnight sitter for the children. Take her to dinner and a movie then surprise her with a reservation at a local hotel that has a spa or hot tub and have a bottle of her favorite wine in the room. Or sometimes just bring her a rose or another of her favorite flowers. Have you ever tried just holding her hand while watching television. Giving her a slow kiss when you pass her in the hall. How about a hug just for nothing. Expressions of love are the only true thing both of you can share.

Chapter 19

Leadership as seen from the Middle

I want to describe what I have learned from over fourty years of my working life. I have worked for large corporations, small corporations, and small businesses and have learned a lot about success and failure in each. I have seen businesses succeed by the greed and avarice or their leaders and seen businesses fail because the leaders wanted to do the right thing but fell victim to reality. I have made money and lost money. I have failed in my personal life making the victories that much sweeter. I have done good and evil. I am no saint but I am also not the devil. I am a man. I have shirked responsibilities I should not have and I have accepted responsibility for things I shouldn't have. I win and I lose but I do them both with such regularity that sometimes I get confused to which I do most. I haven't been a great financial success but I have the love and admiration people I care about and respect. I endeavor to see any situation from both sides and make a some what impartial decision.

This book is some of my thoughts on what true leadership is and why companies now are proporting leadership and teamwork.

What is True Leadership?

In my opinion Leadership is the ability to show others that they can accomplish more than they dreamed and are able to do it on a regular basis. Making the decision to do the right thing and expect no fanfares for doing it, and to leave ideas that make the world better. For ideas are the only thing that outlive us.

Can Leaders be made?

All corporations now understand that leadership is something that can be taught. And it is a good thing to have what they think are leaders working for the company at all levels. Others are under the impression that true leadership is born and can only be encouraged in others. There is truth in both thoughts. There have always been born leaders throughout history. There have also been charismatic people who lead through sheer reason of personality. As William Shakespeare said "Life is but a stage, and we are all but players." Only we can write our own parts if we work for the chance.

Leaders are an important part of any business or group of any kind if they are to be successful, but what is a True leader? Was Hitler a true leader or was he just a person with a point of view that he convinced other people to share. Is Michael Eisner such a great leader or did he just see the problem from a different position and knew what to do. I will try and explain what I mean with an example. Let's say you drive up to find one of your company trucks stuck under an overpass on a rural road in the country. Everyone is walking around talking. Maybe we can force it back out the way it came in or maybe we can get a stronger tractor to pull it through, and then a small child from a nearby home says "Just let the air out of the tires and back it out." Is this child a leader or did he just see the problem from a different position. Of course the child may become a leader but everyone with a good idea is not a leader. A leader may have a good idea but if he is a true leader he will use his leadership to increase his or her probability of success by using the ideas of people with other positions on the situation. There is no shame in using the ideas and inspirations of others to get the job done unless you also keep the credit and rewards for yourself and give only lip service back to the real idea people.

I believe leaders can not be created but can be encouraged and developed. You do not have to be a leader to use leadership qualities, just as you don't have to be a nuclear physicist to understand what a nuclear bomb can do. However when a leader is discovered within a group they must be encouraged and helped to develop those abilities to help the group become successful. Having leadership qualities will not make one a leader. Most leaders don't know they are leaders until a situation shows up that demands they use the leadership abilities. How many presidents of countries or companies show true leadership abilities? How many leaders are we wasting working in jobs well below their abilities because someone else has seniority or are jealous? How many real leaders have been squashed by others with less ability but more power or deception? Why do companies endure people who have no leadership qualities? Because they make money for the company and that is the bottom line. Most companies define success by the bottom line. What other way do they have? Can they say "George is a true leader but lost twenty million last year so, lets' promote him?" No of course not. Profit is king in business and will always be king as long as people need money to survive and live well. This is not a bad or evil thing. We need leaders and we also need business and the two can not be mutually exclusive. In this country we used to make it a point to reward individual effort and new thinking, but there have always been people who are just smart enough to get what someone else has without doing the work. These are not leaders but may be CEO's or Presidents of the companies. As I said Leaders cannot be created but can be developed. Not everyone is a leader or wants to be one. As hard as it may be for some people to understand there is and have always been people with lower expectations and needs as we think. Some people are happy just to work a job a number of hours a week and do nothing more for the company. These people are not less intelligent or less motivated than the leaders but just have a different view of the world, no worse or better that anyone else's. We must accept and be thankful for these people for they are the very backbone of any business. They do most of the real work. Not to say everyone doesn't expect to do better over time with their job but not everyone wants to do what being a leader requires. And not every leader will realize the true greatness of these people. Making a leader is impossible if the person has no leadership ability or does not want to be a leader.

Are leaders created?

Leaders cannot be created. They can be discovered, trained, encouraged, supported and rewarded but not created. If leaders could be created there would be no one but leaders in the world because who wouldn't want to be a leader or make their children one. That is not to say that everyone can't or doesn't have some leadership qualities but they may not be leaders. Leadership is not just a goal but also a trait. Just as a musician may be bad at math or the company president doesn't know one end of a computer from the other. Leadership is not for everyone. If we want good leadership we need to understand what goes into finding a good leader. This can be a daunting task as leaders may show in the strangest and most unexpected places. Most self made millionaires are good businessmen and some may be good leaders but most are not both. Being a good businessman does not make you a leader no more than being a leader makes you a good businessman. Let's take an example of a good leader who is not such a good businessman.

A company makes widgets. They make the best widgets in the world. Everyone wants these widgets. The president started the company by himself in his garage and it has grown to a multi-million dollar operation. He has five hundred employees making widgets twenty-four hours a day, seven days a week excluding holidays. He works a seventy hour workweek and has a seven digit yearly salary. He is a born leader and his employees know he has done every job there at one time or another and has great respect for him and his decisions for the company. He decides to take the company public to raise more capital to build larger and better plants to make widgets and give other people work. The stock sells well and the money rolls in but so does a new board of directors. They are happy and things go well for a time. Then the bottom falls out. Maybe someone developed a better widget or the economy takes a fall and no one is buying new widgets. The president has seen this before and recognizes that things will be rough for a while, but figures that they had made money all those years surely it could afford to lose money for a short time and keep all of his loyal employees. The board does not have a good leader but several good businessmen on it. They decide to sell off 2/3 of the plants to a competitor to help offset losses for the year. Having control they do so. The president has no choice and feels bad, but what can he do? The company shows a profit for the quarter and the shareholders are happy. Only the three hundred or so unemployed people are not. They blame the president for letting them go and feel betrayed. The board gets bonuses and the stockholders get a profit. Then it happens. Widgets are back in style and the company needs to make more than their plants left can make. They loose sales to the very competitor that bought the plants from them. The stock drops and sales are abysmal. The stockholders are complaining and the board blames the president for not leading them. The board decides to fire the president and hire another and they do so. The president has lost almost everything because he was heavily invested in the very stock that has dropped so much and finds himself out of the company. The ex-employees feel he betrayed them and the board of directors have blamed him for not being a good leader. The stock rises on the news of the old president's expulsion and the board of directors hire one of it's own as president. Later in the next year or two the business declares bankruptcy. The board and new president are in a scandal for selling off stock at inflated prices and stealing business resources. The stockholders and the employees are the big losers but the boards of directors are good businessmen and have golden parachutes that land them on easy street for the rest of their lives. The business failed even with a good leader.

Now let's look at a good businessman and a bad leader. The company was established over a hundred years ago by the president's grandfather. They made widgets. They still make widgets but with only 1/3 of the production facilities. Widgets aren't in style right now so he has closed several plants and reduced his workforce. He knows that widgets will come back in style but he can't wait for that to happen so he decides to make crankers also. He retools two old plants to make crankers and hires several hundred employees to do the work. He knows he can get undocumented workers for very little and hires most from those ranks. They work without complaint and as many hours as he wants them to. They turn out crankers at an amazing pace. Sales skyrocket and the money flows. Then it happens. The INS raids one of his plants and takes his workers. The reputation of the business suffers. He hires another group of undocumented workers and makes a decision. He will sell the businesses and retire. He works the people at a breakneck pace to show production and sales increases. Another company with good leaders looks at the plants and decides to buy them. The companies are sold and the company decides that they will do the right thing and help the undocumented workers become legal and spend millions doing so. As soon as they are legal they leave to find better jobs, because now they are citizens. Production decreases due to lack of qualified workers or the cost of qualified workers has increased substantially. The company cannot sell the plants because they are now loosing money. The leaders of the company accept responsibility for the failure and they eventually close all of the plants sending hundreds out of work and regroup to try and start again. The leaders were not good businessmen but good leaders. The company fails again.

These are fictional examples but if we need real ones just look at the newspapers for the last few years Enron, WorldCom and etc. If profit is all that drives our economy the just being a good leader will not be enough. We have to make a group decision that making money any way we can is a recipe for disaster for our way of life.

Leaders are created in a couple of ways. We need to test for leadership and honesty and educate them in the way of the world. We must not give them a picture of the business world as a place of fairness and integrity but as what it can be at its worst. Doing this may increase their chances of succeeding while bringing honesty and integrity back to the world of business. We promote the ideas that a leader is honest and hold him or her to the highest of standards with the goal of being the best leader they can be. We sugarcoat and exalt being a leader as being somewhat of a deity or superior being.

We must teach the reality that evil exists in the business world and it must be fought not embraced.

How can we show what leadership is and how is has been subverted? Just point to the political and the legal system of our country for example. Although most politicians may be or have once been honorable men they have sold out to other interests be they financial or ideological. It has gotten to the point that to meet a congressional representative you have to donate to his re-election fund or something of the kind. Laws are being passed to benefit a small group and most of their representatives and congressmen are either lawyers or rich businessmen. These jobs were never intended to be life long careers but they are now. They even pass laws exempting them from having to obey the laws they pass for everyone else. They vote themselves raises when the economy is in the toilet and cry racist or un-American at anyone or group that points out their failings. They want power not to make a better country for everyone but only for the ones who agree with their ideas. But most people know more about their favorite ball team than what goes on in Washington and that suits the people in power just fine. They will be the first to tell you that you're not smart enough to run you own life. They know what's best for you even if you don't agree.

Having a good leader and a good businessman are more scarce than hen's teeth and almost as fictional. But it does happen and when it does great things happen and great leaders are recognized. But we cannot create a leader we can only appreciate one.

Leadership Training in the workplace

Leadership training in the workplace can be good or bad. Trying to get everyone involved as a leader is not necessarily a good thing. As I have said earlier not everyone is or wants to be a leader. Some just want to follow and be appreciated for the effort. The others are what I want to discuss here. I don't know if I am a leader for I haven't been in a situation where my leadership has been necessary in my business life so much. But I have been to over six years of leadership training. I have sat through talks by people whom I had never heard of before I entered the training sessions and whom I would never come into contact with in my regular dealings. They entertain as well as try to teach. They run successful businesses teaching leadership and teamwork. Please let me know if this sounds like an evangelical preaching poverty from a TV studio while asking for donations from all believers. I find it hard to take a person seriously that has a job that entails making speeches about how important leaders are while making a living making speeches. To me it's like the evangelist that tells everyone money isn't important and faith is everything while wearing a five hundred dollar suit and wearing a Rolex. I want leaders speaking about leadership not inspirational speakers. If you need inspirations from leaders read the works of Thomas Jefferson or Henry Ford people who put all on the line for leadership and sacrifice.

Training people to have leadership qualities is good for a company to allow anyone to accomplish more than they thought they could. I have no problems with teaching people how to make decisions and help the company and themselves. I do have a problem when companies try to tell every employee that they are a leader and that they will be the success or failure of the company. This is a cop out by the upper management like telling a child "If daddy isn't a success it will be because you didn't do well enough in school." Most employees care what happens to their company but have no real power other than doing the best job they can do. Even companies where the employees are involved in stock purchase plans the company management or board keeps more than enough stock to make the employee voting stock almost nill in most cases. Teaching leadership has become a catchword for making the employee responsible for the success or failure of a business. Some employees believe this and work twice as hard to make the right decisions in what they do. This is good for them and the company, but what of the others. They sit and listen to the speeches and how teamwork will make life better for them and everyone else. They espouse what they think is expected of them in response and seem to be willing to do what is necessary to make the company successful. But do they really buy into this? Most don't. They think this is just another ploy to get more work for the same money. Oh sure they don't let on and they do what they must in public but in private they resent the effort to some extent. They have a job to do and all those meetings are if not a waste of time a time to relax and recoup their strength.

Teaching leadership has to take a new direction if we want the average person who works for a living to take notice. Leaders have to meet face to face with the followers. They have to explain and not preach. They need to show more respect for the average employee. They need to also share the wealth. This is not something that is taught in business school. The mantra is pay as little for as much as you can get. Business schools teach ethics and honesty but not sharing. It seems to be alright to pay minimum wage for an employee as longs as they are willing to accept it. Or determine the average wage for a job and with others in the community and state that as the going wage and pay that. Every employer knows good employees are harder to find then hen's teeth but maybe that is because employees are treated as a commodity. They are easy to find where unemployment is high and harder when it's low. They are the last to be increased and the first to be decreased. It's all and good to tell the worker that he is the most important asset a company has but when the profit's fall they all know who will be the first to be gone. In bad time does the upper management take a cut in pay or let the company take a loss for a while. Maybe, but the ones who do are the exception to the rule. In some parts of the south where I live many companies lay employees off on a bi-weekly basis to keep as many people working as possible but others use a lay-off as an excuse when the plant is doing poorly and they need to show a profit for the quarter. My research has shown through interviewing employees on the plant floors of several major textile and carpet manufacturers that the average employee feels that they are being used to fill the coffers of a large and unfeeling corporation. They feel that when things get bad they will be sacrificed on the alter of the bottom line. For the most part they are right but for the wrong reason. Most companies are not heartless and don't like letting qualified employees go. Not for the reason of compassion of humanity for fellow man but because getting qualified employees cost effort and much money. There are even some companies that have a warm feeling for their employees and make sure that they treat them with respect and feeling and take care of them in hard times. These companies usually fail leaving their employees on the street. This seems to be a no win situation for everyone. But this may not necessarily be true.

Most people who grew up in the fifties and sixties have a completely different view of work than today's young. The older generation grew up for the most part where college was considered a luxury for the wealthy, now they are being taught that an education is a right. In the fifties and sixties college almost guaranteed a good job and a future. Now having a degree only says you spent the effort and time to get educated. In trying to make sure our children have a better life then we had we have created a whole generation of self-centered, "Get what you can no matter what" people. I recall my father telling me how he worked for 35 cents a day picking cotton on a farm. I watched my father work hard all of his life to make things better for me and my siblings. I was considered spoiled by my siblings who lived through the hardest times with my parents but how could I know I wasn't alive then. If I carry only one thing from my father it was that you treated people with dignity and honesty and give anything you do all you have.   Leadership was not trained into that generation but they knew what true leadership was.

It wasn't the dot net boom of the nineties but many of the companies started back then still survive and are viable entities. Can we say the same of companies of our generation?

Teaching leadership is a relatively new thing but is it really. Sun-Su's art of war is a complete manual to developing leaders and commanders for war. It set's forth procedures and consequences for almost every action needed in war. I'm not saying that we should adopt any of these measures in training future leaders but just as an example of what was done in the past. It seems most of our leaders until the past fifty or so years came from the military. Until the sixties a military background was an asset if you wanted to be elected to a political office. It now seems to be a determent.

The newfound need for leadership training has expounded a virtual cornucopia of people making a living teaching leadership. They speak most eloquently and entertainingly about how we must all work as one and be responsible for the success of the group endeavor. They juggle and ride unicycles or just smile and spout their prewritten formulas for success. They write books and do videos and sell them for the betterment of all. These people have their place but not where they are. What are their qualifications to teach leadership? Have they run a successful business or campaign of any kind other then a personal public relation campaign? Do they give any knowledge that we couldn't have gotten from someone who is already a success. I feel that we already know what we need to do and these people give the same advise we had gotten from previous generations if we had just listened. What do these people teach, Respect, Pride, Hard work and Honesty. Gee it seems to me my father said the same thing when I was growing up. I feel that leadership training should come from within. Use the leaders in your midst to show the others what is needed. If you have no real leaders in your company then you may want to get outside help but from a successful leader not an entertainer. If you wish, read the books and follow the examples but beware that every business and situation is different and there are no general cures.

You would think from reading the previous that I am against leadership training for all but a chosen few. This is not so. Everyone can benefit from some training in leadership if only for most to see what they can expect from a real leader and how to recognize one. Most people know what teamwork is and how it is beneficial to everyone but they also know that person who is a loner and just wants to do his or her job. One is not exclusive of the other. A loner can do a good job and still help the group without being a buddy to all there. I feel that leadership training can inspire and show the advantages of trying harder and being part of a team. It can encourage leadership traits in people who may not be true leaders. It can increase self image and personal growth. But it will never be a substitute for finding true leaders.

Leadership and Management

Let's take a lesson from a true experience. We all know the shift manager who just seems to get more from their crew than it seems possible. The crew is loyal and will fight to make their crew the best. They have a sense of pride and may even like their work. The management likes what his crew does and wishes all crews were like this one. They decide he would be better if the shift manager had more responsibility over a larger group. He might be able to spread what he can do to other crews. So he is promoted to plant manager. His crew feels betrayed or at least a little disappointed. Of course we know he didn't betray anyone but they think he has. This is a problem of perception. The crew sees him as a member of management now and is at least suspicious if not down right resentful of him. A new shift manager is assigned and he has a completely different way of managing, not worse but different. The crew has a hard time accepting him and work and pride decline. This may resolve itself or it may worsen. The new plant manager has so many people to overlook that he cannot give attention to one crew. Productivity declines and quality suffers. He is soon demoted back to shift manager and he feeling discouraged and somewhat slighted quits and goes to another company. Could this situation have been averted? I think so. Here are my thoughts as to what should have been done.

The shift manager shows himself to be a good leader. He inspires and encourages. His crew respects him and knows what is to be expected of them. If management likes his leadership style they must propagate it. They need this man showing by example what is needed. Offer this man an incentive to help teach others his style. Encourage other shift managers to learn from him while not demeaning their style of management. This manager knows what people want from a leader and can show others how and why what he does works. Most other managers will resist him at first and some will be downright resentful. The true leader will know how to make these people feel more comfortable. However, some will never accept his style. However if only half of the managers adopt some of his ways the return will be great. Offer incentives for a positive response and let the managers incorporate his teachings into their own style. Give this manager's crew a transitional period with him and his replacement and then move the manager to plant leader. His style of management will propagate to the whole plant eventually and productivity and pride will spread. The company will succeeded and they will have promoted a whole new sense of family within the employees making work easier and more productive for everyone. This is a simplistic scenario but it rings true.

Let's go another way. You have a shift manager who has with regularity done below par work. He shows up every day on time and stays until his shift is over. He treats his crew with indifference but no animosity. They have an almost average production and have been doing this for a number of years. You want the crew to do better as other crews have been doing. He has been spoken to on several occasions being encouraged to do better but he hasn't responded as you have wished. He is not disrespectful or Combative, only apathetic. Some feel that he should be fired. Others believe he should just be demoted. There is one other alternative, Leadership Training. If he could just be brought around he would be a great asset to the company without having to train someone to take his position and maybe making things worse. You require him to attend the classes during work hours and after six months or so you check back and find little or no changes in his attitudes. He has watched all of the videos, read the books, and after talking to the trainer you discover he gave all of the proper responses to the questions and even participated in some of the discussions. What went wrong? Believe it or not nothing. He just saw the leadership training as a ploy to get more from him while not getting anything in return. He didn't buy into the concept of the trainer's form of leadership. It might have worked for the others but he didn't believe much of what was said. He heard Honesty, Integrity, Hard Work and Sacrifice, but he already knew about these things and figured that it was a one way street, all on his side. He asks himself "What is the company sacrificing while I work to learn leadership and read and study?" "Am I going to make more money or get more time off for my effort?" he doesn't realize the benefits of what he could learn. He returns to his position and eventually you have to make some decision about him. Either way it's a lose, lose situation.

OK, a bit dramatic but it is a familiar scenario. Let's look at what might have worked for him. I am a firm believer that leadership can be contagious if properly applied. You have the same shift manager and the same situation as before but you decide to try something a little different. You ask around and find another shift leader that is doing a great job and his crew makes an extra effort to do well. They have pride and work to their best abilities. You make a change. You move the apathetic shift leader to the good crew and move the great shift leader to the apathetic crew. You offer incentives either monetary or otherwise to both crews. The apathetic crew sees a good leader and after a transition time where they discover they are not being deceived by the management will get if not enthusiastic at least less apathetic. They learn new ways to do things that make their jobs easier and more productive and they get a sense of pride and accomplishment from their shift leader. They are not intimidated by him and he feels he is doing a good job. I feel people respond to honest and sincere regard for their feelings and workmanship. Now let's go to the other crew. The apathetic shift leader has arrived. He sees the crew smiling and working hard. They almost enjoy their work and eventually after a transition period where he doesn't feel threatened by them will see what they are doing and will adapt his management style to suit them. He doesn't want to make them feel that he is there to make them work harder or a shill for the management. He just sits back for a while and rides alone. But while he is sitting back something happens. He sees something he likes and hasn't had for a long time. He sees people who want to do a good job just for the sake of pride. They are almost having fun at work. They have a sense of camaraderie that has been missing. He starts to go with the flow. He starts to make decisions that are best for his crew and the company which are not at odds with each other. He sees the advantages and makes the adjustments necessary to continue as far as possible with his credo of doing just what is necessary but now just what is necessary is to do better and more but not at a cost to him of anything other than an attitude. You have developed a new person with leadership abilities if not a true leader and have done the best for your company and your employees. There is always a chance this could backfire and the apathetic leader leads the other crew to apathy but I doubt a crew that has pride will fall into apathy if you don't show that you will desert them.

The feeling of the common employee

I feel that upper management fears the common worker too much. If not fear They just don't respect them. They see most as people who want as much money for as little work as possible and the common worker sees the upper management as greedy and self centered tyrants. Both are wrong, to a point. Most people don't like their work. They may not hate it but they don't like it either. Ask any worker in any manufacturing plant if this is where they saw their lives ten years ago and most will say "Of course not." Why is that? Do they want something for nothing? Do the feel that they have just had some bad luck? Do they feel a conspiracy did this to them? Maybe, but most just see what happened as something that was progressive in nature. Most started at the bottom and moved to where they are today. They worked hard and long to get what they have and see their job as a large part of that. They see people doing worse and they see people doing better. They don't spend a lot of time thinking about these things as that can be painful and may even spawn resentment. They show up for work and work hard and when they go home they relax and enjoy what they can. They support the growth of the whole country but don't have a feeling of control of it. They accept the bad as well as the good and try to do better for their children. They are the strength of our nation and we seem to take them for granted. Most feel they work too hard for what they get and are under appreciated. They feel taxes are too high and the United States is the best country in the world in which to live.

It is inevitable for the employee of any company to feel that he is being used and somewhat taken for granted. They see the upper echelon get much more of the pie than they and this makes them feel that they are thought of as an inferior. They want what the others have and can't figure any logical reason why the others have it and they don't. They work just as many hours and just as hard if not harder they the upper management but get few of the perks. They have worked for the company for years and their new boss just got out of school last year. When things are good they get a token, when things are bad they get laid off.

This paints a bleak picture of the American employee but it's not as bad as it sounds. It makes people feel better to think that they are the victims of circumstances beyond their control. They say "There's nothing I can do." or "That's just the way things work." Most don't realize that they have the control to a point and can do something. We as Americans enjoy a higher standard of living than any generation in the past. We have all of the most modern conveniences and technology to keep us healthy and informed. We also have what I consider the lowest morale of any generation in the past fifty years. We expect that we will be treated fairly and the world is not fair. We want monetary success and ignore the really important things. We are envious of the well off and have resentment for them. We want to make the world a nicer place but the world is not a nice place. We are taught to trust in the goodness of humanity and are shocked by the indifference of most people. This was not true just a few generations ago. Since the country moved from an agrarian society to an industrial society work has taken on a completely different definition. Back when everyone grew his own food he was self employed or employed by the land owner and his worth was judged by how hard he worked as an individual. He placed his faith in GOD.

When the industrial age came an employee became a cog in a larger machine. He worked with people he hardly knew and worked on a set hourly schedule. He was paid a fixed amount unless he did piece work and was responsible for only his work. He didn't know how much the company was getting for the finished product or cared unless he needed to buy one. He had pride in his work and worked hard as he was taught by his parents. He saved little if any and was content to be able to feed and cloth his family. He worked a six day week and didn't complain about twelve hour days as that was what he was used to. He saw very little of how the owners lived and knew even less about finances. His wife stayed at home and managed the household.The children went to school and had chores at home to complete. There were no vacations and few days off. He never thought of whether he liked his work or not. It was a job. He hoped his children would have a better life and helped as much as possible to make it happen. He was a simple and honest man.

The employee of today has little in common with this man. They work a fixed schedule usually, but now usually forty or so hour a week (Except Salaried Individuals). They have health insurance and unemployment insurance. They have children in school or college and both family members work. Not to provide food or clothing but to afford the new house, the vacation or new car. They feel used, unappreciated and under paid. They rely on the government to provide for them in times of need. They trust no one and payday is the most important day of the week. They still save little but spend all they earn. They know more about their company they work for than what their kids do while they are at work. They plan their finances and still get deep into debt. They complain about taxes but don't even know who their congressman in Washington is. They work far too hard and far too long and have little to show for it. They place their faith in either the government or themselves. They are the American dream, or is it the American nightmare?

I have performed a personal study of the hourly employee for five years and have asked the same questions to all of them.

1. Why do you do what you do?
2. What do you want from your job?
3. Are you happy with your job?
4. Is your pay sufficient enough for your needs?
5. Do you feel trapped in your present situation?
6. Is the management or owners of your company honest with you?
7. Does the management or owners of your company care about you?
8. Where do you see yourself in ten years?

9. What would or do your parents or family think of what you do?

10. Do you think your better off today than your parents or grandparents?

The results are generally as follows.

1. Why do you do what you do?

The most common answer was "Because I need the money to pay my bills."

The other most common answers were "Because I have done this for years." and I few were "I started out at XXXXX and worked my way here." Surprisingly out of the many people I interviewed I got very few "I like doing what I do." It would seem that the average worker does what he does because he feels he has to.

2. What do you want from your job?

Most said "A paycheck." Others were "A good place to work." And a few "I want to make advancements in my company."

3. Are you happy with your job?

I got a lot of No's but I found that most hourly employees were almost to a person indifferent feeling that that was not a relevant question to be asked about a job. They felt that a job was for the most part neither good nor bad but just something necessary.

4. Is your pay sufficient enough for your needs?

Most said "No." I asked another question in response "How much is enough?" and not as surprisingly most couldn't give me a specific dollar answer other than "As much as I can get."

5. Do you feel trapped in your present situation?

Over eighty percent answered "Yes!" and were emphatic about it. They felt that whether through chance or plan they were where they were without many if any opportunities for change or advancement.

6. Is the management or owners of your company honest with you?

This question had neither a yes or no answer most of the time. They felt that the upper echelon would tell them the truth if it was good for the business otherwise they would be told nothing or a half truth if not a lie.

7. Does the management or owners of your company care about you?

This was another vague area. They wanted to believe the owners or managers of the company cared for them as a human being but they were unsure. Again they believed they were expendable especially in hard times and felt that it might be too much for any company to spend too much effort to care about the individual. They have seen the bad and the good and feel that they have to take care of themselves for the most part because the bottom line is that management will do what is best for themselves and for the company regardless.

8. Where do you see yourself in ten years?

I got a hundred different answers but most boiled down to "I'll be here or somewhere like this unless something drastically changes." They felt they had few options. The older employees that had been doing the same or similar jobs for the last several years had the least thoughts of change, while the younger ones looked for opportunities for advancement with only a small hope.

9. What does your parents or family think of what you do?

"It's my job." was the most popular response. It would seem that most family members are nonjudgmental about what people do for a living if they are in the same social strata. They all wanted their children to do better and have a more professional lifestyle but for the most part everyone was in the same boat.

10. Do you think your better off today than your parents or grandparents?

This was the most surprising part of my questions. For the most part the answer was divided into two sections. They felt better off financially but were adamant about what has happened to our society as a whole and felt the American society was sliding backwards ethically and morally. They felt the family was deteriorating and that money was what everyone wanted at any cost.

I drew these conclusions from the questionnaire. The majority of the Americans (at least in the southernpart of the United States) employees feel they are just a commodity and don't like their work very much. Like machinery or vehicles they are to be used as well as they can be for the company, but are expendable if they become too much trouble or a liability. They can be moved, retooled or disposed of at the whim of the employer. They feel under appreciated no matter how much rhetoric the company espouses of their importance and trapped in their specialty. They want more but don't know how much more. They want opportunities but don't know where to look for them. They work hard and long and for the most part feel they are honest. They want better for their children but don't know exactly what is better. Is it more money or more time with the family? They work a balancing act of work and home life that is unparalleled in American history. They are expected to work any hours necessary and at any time. They are expected to be enthusiastic and thankful. They are the hardest working, least complaining people in America and make almost every advancement made in the last one hundred years possible and not enough can be done for them.

The Employer

Now that we have explored the differences in the employee of yesteryear and of today lets look at the employer.

The company of a few generations ago was much smaller then today. They were mostly a family owned business and had only a few employees. They had a family atmosphere and everyone knew what was going on from day to day. They were self invested in the success of the company. They benefited directly from the company's success. They had a personal relationship with the owner(s). They were involved in most of the important decisions of the company. They were encouraged to have pride in their work and needed almost no encouragement to do so.

The company of today is much different. It usually has several if not thousands of owners and is situated in several locations maybe nationwide. It has hundreds or thousands of employees. They are taught to work as hard and as fast as they can to produce as much as possible asking as few questions as possible. They may only produce a small portion of the entire product and expected to work as many hours per week as the management is willing to pay for. Most employees and management are given the same pay in times of feast as in famine. Pride in work is no longer a necessity belaying to the incomplete nature of their portion of the product. Individual thinking is not encouraged.

This would seem a bleak and solemn nature to today's business but I don't think all businesses are like either of the previous.

Remember the child labor and total lack of safety in the past. The illnesses and deformities caused by chemicals of yesteryear. The harsh and almost slave like working conditions and the small wages and long tedious hours.

The State of Business

The new state of business in this world of today is the conglomerate. The large corporation that have either bought or drove most of its smaller competitors out of the business. They have a management staff of thousands and a workforce of ten times that many or more. They are national if not multinational. They have assets in the billions and as much debt. They provide what they consider good benefits for their employees and a decent pay scale commensurate with the location of the country where they are located. They grow and grow. They are the industry leaders. This is what most people think and for a large part is true. But is it really all there is to it? In the last decade seventy-percent of the new jobs available have been made available by small businesses. Businesses of less than fifty employees have become the new employers. Most are small mom and pop businesses that fill a niche in our society. They provide the products and services that we want and in some cases need. People who own and run these businesses have a somewhat different management style than that or larger companies. Not because the have to but because they can. They can spend more time on an employee and their problems because they have fewer. They can't provide all of the benefits that a large company has but can provide a sense of belonging and importance to an employee because they are important and they do belong. In my experience as a consultant I have found that doing the same job for a small company and doing the same job for a larger company I felt more appreciated by the smaller company. They both paid me the same but the smaller company gave me attention I could never get from a larger company that didn't have the time or the incentive to treat me as important. If I need anything from my job it has to be a sense of pride and importance. I like all other employees want to be treated with respect and honesty and I will return in kind.

I don't want to give the impression that all large corporations mistreat their employees. They are sometimes an underappreciated group. They do provide jobs and a living for many Americans and provide products and services that our country and other countries need. We as Americans are the hardest working, most productive, longest lived people on the planet. We inspire and provide a large amount of the world's products and are the most technologically advanced people on earth.

We also inspire the most jealous and resentful enemies, who seem to have to try and destroy us and our way of life. We are considered Arrogant, Wasteful, Self-important, Self-righteous, and Immoral people on the planet by our enemies and some of our so called friends.

There are many books describing the assent and fall of large corporations. They rise to new heights and fall just as far. There are few that rise and stay up there for many years. We have been accustomed to businesses being there one week and gone the next. With over ninety percent of businesses failing in the first year it's no wonder that we see this as natural. These failures are due to many causes. But most are just businesses that are either too many of that kind or not wanted or needed by the consumer. I find it surprising that there are so many small niche shops in almost any mall in America today. Some sell only one type of item but somehow they survive while others fall by the wayside as snow on the banks of a river. Large businesses are longer in their death throws. They can take years to die and some just change their names and do the same thing as before without the consumer being any the wiser. The larger the business the longer the death takes. If they are run by honest and hard working people the damage is limited by planning. If they are dishonest and greedily managed they will die more quickly and without notice while a few profit enormously by the demise of the company. We have seen the later more frequently in the past few years. Companies who with dishonest accounting practices have left its employees pension funds and stockholders holding bags filled with promises that weren't intended to be honored. While a few leave with amazing severance packages and retirements that would make any world leader happy. This makes the employees feel betrayed and the stockholders cheated and both are true. The government offers no solutions other than to use the same system that gave these people the opportunity to do what they did to try and punish them.

Chapter 20

My Thoughts about other things

Right , Wrong and Making Choices

In today's world right and wrong seem to be subjective. What is right is usually deemed to be what the person believes or can make themselves believe is right. There seems to be a treatice to say that nothing can be wrong if you believe or can convince yourself you are right. I can image that even Hitler thought he was doing the right thing. We rationalize any and all situations placing us in the best light possible in every situation. This is of course human nature. I find human nature to be very convenient and not always the best thing. We humans were given the gift (or curse) of choice by our creator, be he Alah, Jehovah, Shiva or any other name created by man to recognize the creator of all things. Life is a series of choices. From the time we are able to think choices are being made by us from deciding when we are a baby to put everything in our mouths to the choice a person makes to take the life or property of another human. But here is the hang-up. With choice also come consequences and/or responsibilities. If I chose to grab a large hot pepper and bite it I will feel the heat in my mouth. There is no avoiding the result of my action. But if I am a man who wants to take another person's property or life I will try and if I am discovered I have a myriad of options. I can blame my parents for mistreating me as a child. I can blame the school system for not giving me an education so I could afford these things on my own. I can blame society for not making me the kind of person who wouldn't do such a thing. The sad thing is that all of the excuses are accepted by our society. The reason these are accepted are that no one wants to be judged and be found lacking so it is better not to judge at all. Why would I make sure that this person accepted responsibility for his actions when at a later time I might be in a situation close to his and I would not want everyone to judge me? I find this thinking prevalent today. The era of personal responsibility is gone. The era of it's always someone else fault is here. It is taught from the earliest years that it is bad to judge people. If you make judgments you are either, a bigot, a racist or just an ignorant person. Please ignore that in saying these things you are making a judgment. It's OK to make a judgment if you belong to the group that is teaching you not to make judgments. What a crock. Judgments must be made every day of our lives. We must make judgments or we are just victims for anyone who wishes to rule our lives. I make a judgment every day of my life to avoid the high crime areas of a city. I make a conscience judgment every day not to steal or lie. I make a judgment every day not to accept every word that people give me without checking the facts first. I can respect authority without bowing to every whim of the people in authority. I can see the difference between a man who shirks his responsibility as a parent and a person who works so his children may have a home and food. I can see the difference between a man who wants to rule me and a man who wants to represent me. I can tell the difference between a man who was a leader and men who would berate a true leader to make themselves look greater without any actions to prove their greatness. I find people will try to make themselves look greater by using the work and effort of others not as leaders but as leeches. I believe every person has worth. I also believe that worth is for the most part a self judgment. We as parents are allowing our children to be raised by people who may have no other marketable skill other than to teach. I have a great respect for the teaching profession as it used to be. Even as I was going through school the deterioration process was beginning. It has worsened. We no longer teach our children morals at home because if we did we would be guilty of subversion of what teachers are teaching in our schools. It would be great if the world was as the educators wanted. I remember that in high school we had classes to teach young men and women a trade. Now we teach tolerance. We teach that the group right is more important than individual rights. If you make any judgments about anyone else you are basically a bad person. Although you may be bad there is no such thing as evil. Evil is an outdated concept created by religious zealots to scare you into doing the things that particular religion or population segment deems is right. I see the current school system as trying to raise a population of loving, sharing, forgiving, non-judgmental people. I will now identify these people as they truly are and will be, "Victims". If the world would allow these people to live in this way we would be a population of slaves to any society that sets the rights of the majority above the rights of the individual. However the children themselves don't believe this. Look at any school and you will see divisions. You have the jocks, the wealthy, the geeks, the nerds, the cheerleaders, the band members, the hoods, and a lot that don't fit into any category and are ostracized by their so called peers. If you remember when you were young if you were not part of a group you were less than nothing. This holds true somewhat after high school. If you go to college you may become part of a group if you have the time but after graduation you become a part of the largest group in the world if you are lucky, the gainfully employed. Then the grouping truly begins. Do you work in an office or in the plant? Are you a professional person or a laborer? Do you work for a large company or a small one? Can you afford to live in the neighborhood you want to live in or must you settle for less? Will you children be accepted in the right click at school? Do you have the correct car to drive? These are all groups that sometimes you can make a decision to belong to, but what if you have no choice. Granted everyone has a few choices but what if your choices were severely limited. What if you didn't graduate from a prestigious college? What if your skills were only marginal? What if you're not physically able to do certain jobs? Does your worth as a person diminish? Most people would say

145

of course not, but are we being honest with ourselves? We are judged by what we are worth. We don't want to believe that any person should be judged by how much money they have but we do it every day. Would you sell a thousand dollars worth of goods on credit to a man who lives on the street with no visible means of support? You may say that this is an extreme example but let's try one a little closer to home. You want to purchase a home in a new subdivision on the better side of town. You go to the bank and they take your application along with all of the information they say they need to make the decision. Your credit looks alright and your income is marginaly good, but you have three children. The bank decides that you cannot afford the payments because of having to raise three children so your loan is denied. Someone or a group of some ones made a conscience decision not to make the loan just because they think that if the choice came between the mortgage payment and your children you would choose your children's welfare and that on their part would be a bad business decision. Let's try another. You want to move into a neighborhood that has a community housing authority. You want to live there but the committee had a meeting and decided that you did not fit the community and wants to deny you access to the ownership or that property. It is considered a closed community and property can only be sold with the approval of the committee. It would seem that in the real world judgments and decisions are always being made on what other people consider to be your worth. It may not be any way to run a loving and sharing planet but it is all we have. I am not saying that a poor man is worth less than a rich man but the rest of the planet says so. So how can we judge true success? A successful man as far as I am concerned is someone that made a positive and lasting impression on the world. Did I do the right things for my family? Was I honest and held myself to a high standard? Did I do what I know was right? I know every one of us has done things that we are not proud of, but we must never try to justify our mistakes. We must accept the consequences of our actions to show that we are the people that we were put here to be and not cowards hoping that our faults will never see the light of day. I don't criticize people for their mistakes but I will not accept a person who is discovered to do wrong and keeps insisting that it wasn't his or her fault. A child does this in hopes of redirecting anger or punishment and adults do it for the same reason. All of the examples I have given go to prove one thing. Judgments must be made and making them takes courage, information and maybe a little compassion. There is a difference between making a judgment and being judgmental. The latter allows that you are possibly infallible and all of your judgments will be correct. NO ONE is correct all of the time. With only one possible exception there are now nor have there ever been any perfect people. I have also found that tolerance is limited by our training. We tolerate people of other religions as long as it doesn't disturb our sensibilities and since of pride. We are very accepting of other opinions as long as we don't have to live by them. We trust everyone except with our possessions. We hate only the person that is totally deviant or wrong (even if we cannot prove it.) We want lower crime but don't want to make any changes in our everyday lives. We want justice but instead set up a system of laws that have no common sense and give everyone an excuse not to be punished. We want lower taxes but don't want services discontinued or lessened. We want security and are more than willing to give up a few freedoms to get it. This however produces neither security nor freedom. We want to change the world system as long as the oil is still cheap. We hate oppression in other countries but try to silence people we don't agree with. We want political honesty but reward political dishonesty so well. We try to redefine words to suit our current dilemma. We try to circumvent justice but cry foul when our rights or wants are not addressed. We want more prisons but not in our neighborhoods. We want clean water and air but not at the cost of our vacations or our car. We want better things for our children so both parents go to work and let a stranger raise our children not knowing what that person's agenda is. We want all of the things that hard long hours at work get us but loose sight of what is truly important to us. We get angry when our children espouse the things that were taught to them by the stranger taking care of them day to day and do nothing to change the situation because you are getting the material things we want. We watch as our society goes down the proverbial toilet and cannot seem to figure what went wrong, It must be some one else's fault because we were at work making a living and didn't have the time to make any mistakes. We want good representation in government but cannot find the time to vote or research the candidates. We all want love but will settle for sex.

There is a right and wrong and most of the time we can tell the difference. It's wrong to steal, but it has so many rewards. You get something for nothing and you can always rationalize it by saying that you deserve it. It's wrong to lie, but it makes it so easy to avert or delay consequences of your actions. It's wrong to rape, but she was just asking for it. It's wrong to kill, But that S.O.B. shouldn't have made me angry. It's wrong to criticize someone we don't know, but look at the way they are dressed and what they eat. It's wrong to persecute someone for their religion, but those people don't believe in the one true god as I do. It's wrong to hate someone because of the color of their skin or nationality, but those people are not really people are they. The first thing you have to do before you do something to someone is to decide they deserve what is coming and that you are right in doing what you are about to do. I am sure that every person in prison at one time or another was or is sure that they don't deserve what is happening to them. I am sure that almost every woman pregnant out of marriage thinks that they didn't do anything to deserve this. I am sure that almost every man that is having a child out of marriage thinks that this is her problem not his.

Most problems of mankind come from one source. Not Satan, or another evil entity although I say he has a hand in it. It comes from making bad or ill informed decisions. No one wants to held accountable for their bad decisions.

Let's take a chain of decisions that people make and follow them to their logical and invariable conclusions.

149

You graduate high school. You now have to make a choice to college or to work.

If you choose college you will have to study hard and may have to sacrifice personal time and pleasure for your studies. Besides you can go to work for your dad's plant and make good money. So college is not the option you choose, besides you want to marry that one special girl and start a family. So now another choice, get married or wait. You decide not to take a chance that someone else will get the girl of your dreams so you get married after you have worked a few months and have enough money to move out on your own. You now have it all or so it seems. Your wife has just told you that she is going to have a baby. You will be happy having a little one around and it will look just like you. Of course it's a girl and looks like her mother. After a couple of years of marriage and two more children you feel that life may just be passing you by a little so you turn to a female co-worker for some simple conversation. Now you have another choice, continue the relationship with the female co-worker to its logical end or stop it where it stands and go home. You figure no one will know and it's not serious so you continue. Several months later the co-worker is either angry with you or pregnant. Your wife finds out and you are living alone again in a cheap hotel or trailer if you are lucky. Of course it was your wife's fault because the relationship didn't work out and that bitch of a co-worker is also to blame. Your life is not a happy one. You're paying child support for children you rarely see and your job is getting to be a joke. You work ten to twelve hours a day and get to keep very little of your pay. You look back on your life and finally decide that the legal system and society have ganged up on you to keep you in this situation, poor and powerless. You have decided that fate has played a cruel trick on you and you are helpless in the tide of time and circumstances. But none of this is your fault. Now this may seem like I am making huge assumptions and for sure not all people will come to these ends but far too many do. Look at the decisions this person made.

1. Not to go to college. Granted college isn't for everyone but everyone needs to take advantage of any education or training they can get while they are young and unattached.

2. Get Married right out of high school, If you are truly in love a year or so won't make enough difference in your love. However if it doesn't last it probably was a good thing you weren't married.

3. Getting involved with another person. If you did make the commitment to a marriage you must make every effort to make that marriage work. I know from experience that this isn't always possible but think twice before you go this route.

4. Have a child. A child is a lifetime commitment and will take up more of your time and resources than you can ever imagine. A child is not just something to show and be proud of they are a gift from God and then only hope we have for any future.

5. Blame everyone but yourself. <u>YOU</u> made each and every decision that has brought you to your current situation. Maybe the other people had some input to your situation but the decisions were all yours. You didn't want any further education, you didn't want to wait for that girl. You wanted the other woman, you decided your marriage wasn't enough and wanted more.

Making correct choices are sometimes the hardest choices to make and other times they are the easiest. Taking responsibility for the choices you make is what will make you a better person and a more respected individual. It will also make your life a lot less complicated.

So much for my treatise on right and wrong and I will leave you with a few quotes. None of these are mine but they make a lot of sense.

"There can be no justice as long as laws are absolute,"

"There is always less to remember if you tell the truth."

"The facts and the truth are seldom the same."

"Right is the choice you make that you can convince yourself of"

"If you feel bad after you have done something it was probably the wrong thing to do."

"If it ain't broke.. don't fix it.

"Youth is wasted on the young."

"Klattu verada nikto"

Would Jesus drive an SUV

The title of these next pages were taken from a news story I heard while driving to work one morning and it seemed so ludicrous that I just had to use it for something. You might as well ask if Jesus would own a DVD player on his computer. I don't claim to be a biblical scholar although I have spent many of my fifty years of life searching for the truth and researching many different religions. I have had many discussions with many religious leaders from Baptist ministers to Jewish rabbis. I discount no person for their beliefs and I accept no religion at face value. If your religion is the only true religion prove it to me without trying to make me believe that if I don't believe the way you do that I am doomed to some kind of eternal torment. There may be a one true religion on our planet but as long as religions are run by men there are going to be a lot of errors made in the interpretation and execution of God's word. I do believe in a God, being mainly a man of science I cannot discount that anything as complex and intricate as our universe could be created by pure chance. I don't accept the premise that 1,000,000 monkeys typing on typewriters would eventually write the complete works of Shakespeare. Because while typing the monkeys would defecate on the typewriters, destroy most of them by sheer force of typing. And so forth. I do believe however that God does nothing without a plan and a purpose. We might not see the plan or see any purpose but he does. So take my thoughts with a grain of salt and make up your mind as to where I may be right and where I may be mistaken.

Would Jesus Drive an SUV?

This was a question asked by people whom I figured had more time on their hands that they needed. On the surface it would seem to be a somewhat silly question raised by people who figure that we are destroying our planet for the fun of driving a large automobile. But I think that the problem with this question goes much farther than this. For Years it was a good thing to ask before we made a decision "What would Jesus Do?" In most social circumstances this may be a reasonable question, but remember that Jesus was also a man and as much as we were taught by our elders he was perfect and without sin, the scriptures say that he was also a man. He had all of the human frailties. He got Hungry, Happy, Sad, Sleepy, and Angry. He had to have all of the problems that go with being a human or the sacrifice he was to make would mean nothing. I have always wondered when he found out about who he really was. I mean think about it. You are told that you are the son of the creator of the universe. You will suffer and die at the hands of the human race. You will however rise from the dead in three days and live forever. And some ask the question that if he knew he was going to rise from the grave and live forever was the sacrifice really that great. I mean if he was God Incarnate did he really have anything to fear from these puny humans. I am of the belief that he may have known who he was but was not told the complete picture until the last minuet. Did he not ask in the garden if the cup might be taken from him if it be God's will? This would seem to be the question of a man afraid of what was going to happen to him, maybe afraid of the unknown fate awaiting him. It would take great courage to face the torment that was coming not being sure of the outcome. We are told every Sunday about how he rose from the grave and will meet us in heaven but I have yet to meet a person living that is not somewhat afraid of death. Many say that they are not afraid of dying but is this really true? Men of faith are told not to be afraid of death. That it is just a temporary sleep. But without the luxury of first hand knowledge we will still fear the unknown. I think God made us this way so that the faith that we carry will have some meaning. If we didn't fear death we might seek the release so that we would be in heaven with our family already past. God gave us a healthy fear of death so we would carry out the things we have to do here on earth. I will speak more to this later. Death however is the great equalizer. It is one of the things that all persons rich and poor will have to face. I am not ashamed to say that I have a fear of death. I don't know if it is because I love this life so much or that I am afraid of the unknown. I personally believe that there is life after death and that someone is watching over me. I cannot prove any of this but to believe anything else just doesn't make any kind of logical sense. Some say that death is the end. I say science and theology say otherwise. As any first year physics student knows Energy is never destroyed only transformed. If you start a fire you may burn the wood but the heat from the fire it created is never gone only dissipated into the universe. So I believe that our essence (Our Soul if you will) will never be destroyed it will only be transformed.

The Rift between Science and Theology

There has always been a discussion between men of science and men of theology about who is correct. I surmise that one cannot exist without the other. Men of god say the science is subverting the will of god and science says that god may not even exist. Both views I believe are wrong. Science as I see it was created by god to validate his existence by letting mankind discover how he works. And I also believe religion was established by god to let mankind accept by faith what they have yet to discover through science. One of the things I have heard by studying science was a beautiful thought, it was said "The mind of god is music made in multiple dimensions of hyperspace." I will not get into the theory of quantum science or string theory to try to explain this thought but it does one thing for me. It shows that science can recognize God and still search for the answers. As I have mentioned earlier I believe that god has a plan and a purpose. The complete plan is not evident as we cannot see but our small piece. But I believe the purpose is for mankind to grow and learn so that the existence of god can be determined without reservation of doubt by the means of faith and knowledge. I do not discount faith as the force behind any religion but if faith is subverted then it becomes a device of evil and injustice. I believe more crimes and atrocities were done in the name of religions than were done by all of the other reasons that have plagued our planet. It seems that any religion of the world has to proclaim itself as the one true religion. If you don't follow the rules set out by this religion, or that religion you are doomed and do not even deserve to live. It seems strange that all religions have a doctrine of not killing anyone for any reason and that every religion in existence condones or supports the death of someone that does not belong to that religion. There are radicals in every religion, even the religion of science. So what is the one true religion? Is there a one true religion? What is the difference between religion and faith? How do we always seem to be the chosen ones and not the other religions? Why are we so intolerant of other religions? Why are religions so violent? What can we do to fix the problems?

All very hard questions and there are no simple solutions but here are some of my thoughts.

Is there one true religion?

I seriously doubt it. I have seen and visited many different religious ceremonies and services. Most teach the same things in very different ways. Some are using ceremonies and religious route to press a structured faith others believe in freeform and very animated services. Some sing very organized and others just sing with fervent zeal. There does seem in my opinion to be one thing missing from most services. Joy. It seems to me that we should be full of joy and happiness when we gather to celebrate God and his magnificence. Instead we try to cajole and scare the people into accepting our way of thought and organization by showing them the errors of their ways even if they didn't know they were wrong. By telling them that if they don't have faith as us they are doomed. If their faith is not our faith then they cannot be right with God. Look at the first few rows of the church pews, do you see joy or smugness. Is there an air of happiness or an air of self-righteousness, an air of forgiveness or an air of silent retribution yet to come? I have rarely been at a service where the goodness and joy of god's love is exalted with no strings attached. Where the minister is preaching love and forgiveness instead of sin and retribution, where judgment is left to the creator instead of the leaders of the church or it's paritioners.

If I want to feel real joy all I have to do is to look into the eyes of my grandchildren or see the sunrise of another day. These are the true miracles that prove the existence of a creator. If you can't enjoy a beautiful sunrise or sunset, or the smile and laughter of children then you are missing one of the true expressions of god's love to us. If when you look into the eyes of someone you love and cannot see beyond the physical being you are missing half of the beauty of that person. If having more than your neighbors is more important than talking to or spending time with your children then humanity is at a disadvantage. Maybe the religion that we all need is not organized as we now have it. I have nothing against houses of god. I am sure that they are necessary in god's plan to get people together. But I feel that the house is only as joyful as the people in it. Remember Jesus never had a church that he personally organized or built. He left that to his disciples and other followers.

What is the difference between religion and faith?

This is a very hard question with a simple answer. These are my thoughts.

Religion is a set of doctrines developed by men to help them represent what they feel to be the correct way to worship the creator.

Faith is believing in things that cannot as of this time be proven by any physical means that aids in the belief in a supreme being.

In my opinion faith is much more important than any religion. Jesus did not say "Your Religion has set you free." Jesus spent a lot of time explaining to people that faith is important. Why would a creator want the faith of the people of the universe? Surely he didn't need the faith to exist or to do what he wanted. I believe that the creator gave us faith so that we would not see everything in existence to be supernatural and therefore beyond our comprehension. I feel that god eventually wants us to understand everything in the universe. Just because we understand everything doesn't mean we can reproduce it and become GOD ourselves. He wants us to know why and how he did what he did. It makes it very easy for me to exalt god when I see all of the intricacies he created just so we can exist on this planet. How every plant and animal exists to prove a point. How every scientific discovery shows the ultimate wisdom of the plan. Having faith is like having the expectation of something wonderful to come. Knowing that maybe god has some reason for you to exist. That maybe we were meant to be more that we are now. That eternity is something to be anticipated with joy and not feared.

Why Is Our Religion The Only Real One?

I think that it s fundamental for every human to believe that he is almost always correct in any judgments that we have to make. If we didn't feel this way we would never be able to leave our homes in the morning knowing that we would inevitably do something that would kill us. In religion there is no stronger doctrine than "We are the right religion and we know what god wants from us." If our religion is so right way doesn't everyone believe the way we do. "OH Wait! They must be ignorant of the right way and it is my duty so show them the error of their ways. If they won't change then they must be evil and therefore controlled or destroyed".

Most of us who live in any religious society are taught from birth that god wants us to believe in him and that there are certain ways that we must do this. Go to church or synagogue, Lie prostrate on the floor facing Mecca and chant, Get on you knees and pray for forgiveness, or maybe just confess your sins to another person in private. I find it hard to believe that the creator of the universe needs any of our groveling or pious demonstrations. Fall to your knees if you feel you need to pray that way. But please when I pray don't tell me that God won't hear my prayer because I am not in a prostate position. I tend to do my praying in private. I feel that my prayers are for God and not anyone else. If God hears my prayers why should I care what other people think? My prayers are for God and God only. I pray usually several times a day and I try not to let a day go by without thanking god for what I have and for my family. I can do this while driving or sitting at my desk. I don't need a cathedral or church for this. Praise the creator in what you do and you will do it well.

Why are we so intolerant of other religions?

It would seem that every religion preaches tolerance of other people until the topic of belief comes up. Religion is the one subject in which there is no room for compromise. The Muslims believe all Christians are as animals, Christians believe the Buddhists are heathens, Buddhists believe all other religions are just silly; Jews don't believe that Jesus was the Messiah and so forth and so on. Who is right? Everyone and No one. As far as I can see God doesn't sanction any one religion. God gave man the ability to create laws. Some good, some bad but laws are the foundation of any society. They tell us what to do in certain circumstances. The bible teaches that Moses got the Ten Commandments from God on a mountain. As true as this may be the laws given were mostly common sense and most were being followed for thousands of years prior. Killing and stealing were always bad things. Adultery and lying were also known to be bad. The one new thing added was not having another god before him. This brought all of the believers into one camp and solidified their power base. I believe myself there is only one supreme creator and maybe Moses did get the laws from god, but this was the basis of all future laws governing people even to today. I cannot find one section in the bible where Jesus or God says "Here is the one true faith". Jesus preached love and forgiveness wherever he went. No building was ever created just so Jesus could preach to the people. He made use of the Synagogues and Hilltops as well as the Seashore and Fields of the countryside. He lived off of the generosity of the people that he met and demanded nothing for himself. He chose followers and did his best to educate them. He spurned no one and accepted any person of any religion without criticism of their belief or nationality. He however was human and did show this. Did he not get angry at the money changers at the temple? Did he not change water into wine at a wedding? When he did rebuke anyone I believe it was with quiet words and was very personal. I also have a feeling that he was tempted by women but realized that to make that kind of a commitment meant heartache and pain for his spouse and children so decided not to do it. I don't have any facts to back this supposition up but I believe that he had all of the feelings that we have today or else he could not understand us as well as he did. But what of the followers of Mohamed, are they just fooling themselves? In today's environment we Americans see most Muslims as enemies and just plain crazy people. This leads to my next question.

Why are some religions so violent?

It seems today that religion has become an excuse for violence but we have to take a larger view of the situations. Down throughout history religion and politics were close. So close in fact that some races of people are still defined by their religion. Countries have established state religions. Religions have established control over several countries. And both have ruled their citizens with an iron hand. In my opinion it all boils down to one thing, Power. Power over other peoples lives. We say that we live in a free society and for the most part this may be true. We try to keep our government and our religions separate. But what kind of country would we have if we didn't have faith. And faith is not the same as belief. I may believe I am doing the right thing but my belief may be wrong, however my faith is in a higher being that will eventually show me the correct way. Our country was founded by people who felt persecuted by the established religions of Europe only to come to this land and try to change the religion of the natives and when that failed, they tried to eradicate them as much as possible. People think that freedom of religion is not the same as freedom from religion.

What religion on this planet has not tried to convince or convert people of other religions? If this fails then they look upon these beings as somewhat sub-human or ignorant of the facts. What religion has not warred against another religion to exert control over its people? Does it seem strange that one religion owns the largest bank on earth? What is the difference between a dictator telling his people how to live and a religious leader telling the world what is correct? Why do we think of our ministers and religious leaders as always correct? If you don't believe what I say try and correct a minister when he is wrong during a sermon. If you are not thrown out then and there you will have to leave quickly after the sermon to protect your well being. We have been taught that men of god have a special insight into important matters. Is This True? I believe that God can steer the hand of man but I don't believe that any person who thinks he knows what god wants may be fooling him or herself and others. I don't think that the words of god need that much interpretation. I try to steer clear of people who have God's 800 number. I get scared when such people gain power in our government. There is nothing more dangerous than a person who thinks he or she is doing the "Will of God". We get angry when the Muslim community kills and says that it is the "Will of God" but we rejoice when any country with a different form of government falls and makes us more powerful in the world. We Americans may have the best form of government on earth today but do we have the right to make everyone see this. Is it alright to liberate (another word for conquer) a country because we feel threatened by them. Is having a weapon that can harm our people enough reason to topple a government and replace it with someone we like better, maybe. After all we are supposed to protect our own people and where do we say "OK we will protect you until someone else has the strength or ruthlessness to take us over." It is a complicated question. There are a lot of holy writings showing wars that God has wanted fought, at least which was what was relayed to us. I think that man has injected his own feelings and interpretations to the scriptures over the years to try and improve them. It's wonderful to think that right will always prevail over wrong, but we know better. Evil is a force as prevalent as righteousness. To think that everything will work out for the best is naive. If this were so why did millions have to die in the concentration camps in World War II? Why do people starve to death in a country where the rulers live like kings? Why are children beaten to death and starved while the neighbors ignore the problem? There is a saying "It is evil enough if good people do nothing while evil prevails." It seems that some religions teach that it is the responsibility of all of its followers to sacrifice their lives in the name of destroying anyone not protected by their doctrine. It also seem to me that the ones sending these people out seem to be immune to their own doctrine, for as soon as they are face to face with the situation they run and hide to tell their followers that they must sacrifice more to protect their religious leaders. How many sixty year olds do you read about caring a bomb into a crowded restaurant or Mall? These people take advantage of the religious zeal of their followers to solidify their power base. Not that we don't have our own religious leaders living off of the work of their followers, but we don't seem to get the kind of followers willing to sacrifice all for their belief that all other people must be wrong and therefore killed whenever possible. Is Violence the answer? It seems to work for some. Until September the 11th did most Americans know who Osamma Bin Laden was, Or who The Taliban were. Most

Americans knew such people existed but they wouldn't dare attack us on our soil. Violence has worked because we feel we must respond to violence either with violence or flexing of our global political muscle. These usually work, but what can you do to a person willing to give their lives because someone with influence over them tells them that if they die in the act of killing unbelievers that heaven and a rich reward awaits them after death. I relate this to the situation of coming face to face with a mother grizzly protecting her young. You can run but sooner or later she will catch up with you. You could try to threaten her with your knife but she really isn't scared. You could yell very loudly as you were taught and maybe she would run except for her having cubs, or you could take your gun and kill her in front of her cubs leaving them helpless.

I represent a zealous religion as the cubs and they have a long memory and will feel that you killed their mother unjustly and will want revenge. Now we have to deal with a whole new generation of killer bears. This is basically what has happened in certain parts of the world. We try to stamp out violence with like violence and the only way that anyone will win is if one side is completely destroyed. Using any political process makes the assumption that both people want peace. If either is using the process to gain an advantage then the process must fail and the violence must increase. The only way in this situation that peace can be achieved is for one side or the other to have an ally that has enough power to totally erase the opponent from the face of the earth, and the aggressor sees that they will lose and therefore will negotiate. This makes peace tenuous at most because when the threat of force is removed the violence will resume. All this done in the name of Religion. I believe that God never wanted us to kill another human for any reason except self defense. I say any religion or people that pretends to preach love and forgiveness and then promotes killing in the name of their religion will pay the ultimate sacrifice and will eventually be removed from the earth and hopefully purged in the pages of history and forgotten by all peace loving people.

Now I will discuss what I believe is evil in The United States. It seems that evil has a stronghold in America today. Our representatives don't represent us they represent their own interests. The laws are written to help a few and powerful. Accountability is for no one. The purpose of government is to provide all of our needs. It seems that the main use of government is to redistribute the wealth of a free nation to its entire people whether they deserve it or not. You are entitled to whatever the politicians can reap for you. Remember the government is the only institution in the United States that can enforce its will at the barrel of a gun. Letting zealots (Political or religious) get control of the government is the same thing as giving one person or group of people the rule of us all.

What can be done to fix the problem?

I'm not sure the problem can be fixed with the state of mankind today. As long as any person or group of people feels that they have the right and obligation to tell other people how that should live then these situations will continue. I have always disliked anyone who seemed to tell everyone what the problem was without having at least somewhat of a solution so I will give my thought on what I think may help the situation. The only thing that will make these people seem as foolish as they really are is to make sure that every person on the earth has what they need to exist in peace. I don't mean make everyone rich but make sure that every human on earth has food, clothing and shelter as well as dignity. It is much harder for someone to influence another if he can't show a basic injustice toward that person. This seems impossible to schieve in today's world and I don't see it changing in the foreseeable future. There is no answer that will work until the hearts of man are changed so we all have respect and understanding of every religion and respect for all individuals.

Should we all be just like Jesus?

It seems like a simple question. Why would we all not try to be the most perfect person that ever lived on earth? Living our life just to tell the rest of the world about our father in heaven, but is this what god really wanted us to do. I believe that God has another plan for us. In today's world Jesus would probably be seen as a religious fanatic. Let's look at this from the angle of the secular world of today.

1. Jesus was a carpenter who left his job to travel and talk to people of different areas of his world making him and unemployed hobo or at least a traveling evangelist.

2. He had no earthy possessions so he would be considered a vagrant in our society.

3. He had no permanent home of his own making him homeless.

4. He lived off of the charity of others making him a beggar in our society.

5. He preached a flavor of religion detrimental to the established religion and Government making him a troublemaker or a traitor.

6. He traveled with a group of people taking their orders from him and blindly following him making him a gangleater or the leader of a religious Cult.

None of these things were true at the time he lived, but are we really to try to be like Jesus. I believe that we have a purpose in this world and God gave each of us a talent. I don't think that God wanted billions of evangelicals. He gave us the talent to be what we are and the talent to make this world a better place. He knew we would need Doctors, Machinists, Construction workers, Computer programmers and yes even Lawyers. Every person on this planet has a skill. All we have to do is to make that skill work for us and mankind. Our skills are part of the plan God has for us and when we use our skills for the betterment of mankind everyone benefits. There is no such thing as an unimportant job. Sometimes we think that just because we are not the most important person in an organization we are just a cog in the big machine. This may be true but you take any machine that uses cogs and remove one even a small one and see what happens. Our society tends to judge a person's worth by their education and financial standing. I feel we are making a grave mistake when we do this. If you use the same standard towards Jesus you would find him severely lacking. A man must define his own value. A man has value to his family that cannot be measured in any tangible terms, for what is love and respect worth. The value of any person is in his own mind and heart and the hearts of the ones that love him. Not to discount people who have made major contributions to our world such as Leonardo Da Vinci, Einstein, or Mother Teresa. These people made a huge impact on this world and deserve our respect and admiration. However we cannot also discount other people, like the man who picks up your garbage, the plumber who fixes your sink or the auto mechanic who gives you mobility. There is an old saying "There is never a job too small for the man only a man too small for the job." I know everyone wants a good job that pays a lot of money but if money would make you a good person then greed would not be a detriment but an asset.

God also gave us the family. I will not try to define what constitutes a family but knowing you have someone who cares for you and loves you for no other reason than you exist is comforting. I came from a rather large family and always seemed to have closeness to the other members of my family that some people seem to miss. Jesus also had a family. No not a wife and children because I believe if he knew what was coming he didn't want to have them suffer as he knew his mother would. I think God created the family so we would know the love he has for us on a personal level. If God thinks of us as his children then having children ourselves gives us a glimpse of what he feels for us. If we have a wife or husband maybe this is a symbol of how God feels toward his followers in truth and peace. I think God gave us the church for us to expand our family and to include people who may not have a family of their own so they may feel the love and joy of a real family. When we gather for special occasions as a family maybe this represents how God wants us to join together at church in happiness and joy to show our appreciation for what he has given us. I may be wrong but I feel that if I am, God will forgive my misunderstandings as I forgive my children's and grandchildren's mistakes. If God is who I believe him to be then we as a race must rethink why we are like we are and try to improve ourselves as much as we can in one lifetime. I hope I can spend eternity after death exploring all of the beauty and diversity of our universe with God as my teacher and friend.

Chapter 21

Now for a short discussion about Cloning

      I jump into this as an unrelated subject. There has been a lot of discussions about cloning and the moral and ethical repercussions of the science of duplicating animals and people. Most religions don't believe an animal has a soul so cloning must not be a problem except with humans. Most religious people seem to think that this kind of science is playing god with humanity and we don't have the right to do this. Science says that the moral issue is inconsequential and that the science of cloning will lead to a better life for all mankind. I personally don't fall into either of these categories. My thought is that cloning is a science that has come. The Genie is out of the bottle and if we don't find some way to compromise we will have a large amount of outlaw cloning done in the world by not so nice people for not so nice purposes. I believe that only God can bestow a soul and science can only build a home for the soul. It is much like a construction company building a home and then someone else has to occupy the house and make it a home. If God gives the clone a soul then we must treat the clone as a full fledged member of mankind with all of the rights and responsibilities that go with it. Cloning a person does not make the clone an exact duplicate of the person only a genetic duplicate. A person natural born or cloned is the sum of all of the experiences that they have had since birth and these can never be truly duplicated. If however we as a people decide to treat clones a property and can do with them as we will then we are no better than the slave owners of the past who abuse their power and think that some people are inferior to others because of their birth status or color. I feel pretty confident that we won't fall into this trap again. Remember also that the scientists who are doing cloning are creating nothing. To create a clone a scientist must have living tissue with which to work. I would worry if a scientist walked into an empty room and said "Let there be living cells.", and then walked out with living cells. Only God can create life all science can do is try to duplicate after the fact. I have heard people who say that within twenty-five years science will be able to transfer the essence and thought patterns of a person from an old body to a new cloned body. I find this hard to believe. We have only begun to start to map the human psyche and really have no knowledge why or how it works. If this is at all possible I think we would probably have a limited power to do so. I think that our minds are irrevocably attached to our soul and only God can bestow a soul on a being. I will not get into the discussion of when a group of cells becomes a human. Some say that an egg and a sperm when they meet is a human, Others say not until 12-24 weeks , still others say not until it takes its first breath out of the mother's womb. I just don't know and feel that if a baby can be brought to term then we need to do just that. A life is a terrible thing to waste.

In Conclusion

Just as a conclusion to these writings I want to say that I have found that at my age I love my life. I was never as rich or as successful as I wanted to be, because maybe if I were I might not have been trying hard enough to be a better person. Having been in love with the same woman for 25 plus years I find that I am very lucky to have what I possess. I have done a lot of things I shouldn't have done and I know that I have and will have to explain myself for my actions. I find it hard to believe in a god that will punish anyone for eternity for any actions no matter how misguided unless true evil was involved. I also find it impossible that this universe has come to pass as a result of coincidence and or strictly evolution. I believe in a god that is, loving, forgiving, gentle and understanding as he was the one who created all of these traits in the human kind. I love my children even when they don't do what I think is right and no love is greater than the love for my grand-children. I have developed many skills that I hope to pass to future generations and I hope I am leaving a legacy of beauty and hope for my family and other people whom I have had the pleasure of meeting and getting to know. Being a mortal man I fear what I don't understand so death looms large on the horizon for me. I fear that maybe my conceptions of the universe were skewed and not to the liking of the creator (this is where the forgiving and understanding comes in) but what can I do about how I see the universe. I fear leaving my family and friends for what would a person be without these except a failure. I try to have no illusions about myself but every person on this planet wants to be thought of as someone special and I feel special because of the people that make me feel that way. I hope that I have made others in my life feel the same way. If my life is to have any meaning it must be that I have always tried in the end to do what I know is right.

If I were to give a short bit of advice that would put someone on the path to enlightenment (as if I am enlightened)

1. Be happy with yourself and make sure that you can forgive yourself, because it's impossible to truly forgive anyone else if you can't forgive yourself.

2. Try to manage any anger and regrets you have with your life. We all make mistakes, the real challenge is not to compound our mistakes with rationalizations or excuses, but to not repeat them

3. Love as many people as you can and love without conditions, because if there are conditions it's not real love.

4. Do the right thing. I don't mean the expedient thing but what your heart knows is right.

5. Treat your spouse as if they were the best part of you, because they are.

6. Let your children be what they were meant to be. Guide them, give advice when asked and punishment only when necessary. Make sure that they know right from wrong and love them without bounds or conditions.

7. Make your family the first priority in your life as god has made us his highest priority.

8. Keep self pity to a minimum and accept the consequences for your actions. Don't be a coward.

9. Realize that life is a gift, We must enjoy the small things in order to be at peace with ourselves and our creator. Don't forget to smell the flowers and also look for the beautiful sunrise or the golden sunset. See the clouds make shapes or the stars twinkle in eternal night. Look in your children's eyes and see a new universe. Or look into your spouse's eyes and see eternity. Life is good.

10. Finally remember the words of a wise man from The Wizard of Oz. "You are not judged by how much you love, but by how much you are loved by others."

End